The Upside of Down

The Upside of Down

How Chaos and Uncertainty Breed Opportunity in South Africa

Bruce Whitfield

MACMILLAN

First published in 2020
by Pan Macmillan South Africa
Private Bag x19
Northlands
Johannesburg
2116
www.panmacmillan.co.za

ISBN 978-1-77010-725-0
e-ISBN 978-1-77010-726-7

Editing by Russell Martin
Proofreading by Wesley Thompson
Design and typesetting by Triple M Design, Johannesburg
Cover design by publicide
Author photograph taken on the rooftop of Discovery HQ by Abigail Javier

For Cameron & Scott
Make your stories matter

Contents

Preface

'You may encounter many defeats,
but you must not be defeated.' – Maya Angelou

It's my 'Wall of Worry'.

I look at it now: an extraordinary array of books detailing the failings of South Africa and its corporate and political leaders over the last decades. The titles stare malevolently from the shelves. There's Jacques Pauw's *The President's Keepers*, Rob Rose's *Steinheist*, Pieter-Louis Myburgh's *Gangster State*, RW Johnson's *How Long Will South Africa Survive?* ... and a slew of many other similar doomsday books, whose rate of publication has escalated in recent years. Together they tell a story of a country on the verge of self-destruction. It's a wonder there is a country left to speak of.

What in fact has ensured that South Africa has not collapsed in on itself?

For one thing, civil society has been pivotal in fighting for the rights of citizens, especially the marginalised, and forcing the hand of government, often through the courts, to acknowledge its responsibility, its duty of care, and its obligations under the constitution. The judiciary too has been crucial in steadfastly upholding the rule of law and ensuring that the hard-won constitution has remained the lodestar of our society. Moreover, without a free media highlighting some of the worst excesses of public- and private-sector malfeasance, the South African story would be very different too.

But there is another story to tell as well. It's about the role that many companies and some of their bosses play, often unseen in the public domain, in guiding, cajoling and influencing the country and its leaders in the pursuit of a sustainable future.

This is often derided as a new form of state capture, but as delegates to the 50th World Economic Forum gathering in Davos in January 2020 were reminded, there is a complex interrelationship between government, business, labour and civil society which creates a series of checks and balances that occasionally do veer out of kilter, but generally serve to keep all interest groups in hand. Just as business requires political stability and policy certainty to thrive, governments need profitable businesses to keep creating jobs that provide the growth that pays the taxes that can service the needs of voters. Straddling all of the vested interests is a range of civil society bodies, acting for a multitude of interest groups, all seeking to influence the way in which nations develop and striving to keep key role players honest. It's imperfect. But it's the best system developed so far.

The political settlement of 1994 not only brought democratic rights and freedoms in South Africa, but it also provided the conditions in which the economy could flourish and businesses could contribute to the economic growth of the country and the building of a better life for all. Foreign investors, who for years had shunned South Africa because of the apartheid ideology, began to return and to invest; while local conglomerates, which had been built up by virtue of the fact that they had nowhere else to invest their capital, began to unbundle and spread their wings internationally. There was a groundswell of optimism and fresh energy as bold entrepreneurs saw new opportunities in both the domestic and global environments and created new enterprises which contributed to job creation and overall economic growth. For the first decade or so of the democratic era, there was a strong sense of hope that South Africa might just make it.

But that sense of optimism has been eroded in recent years and South Africa is now running out of time and money. The ANC-led government is stuck in an invidious position in that it has made big promises to an increasingly frustrated electorate and, unless it can conjure up growth quickly, it will not have the financial resources to make good on its pledges to voters. Unemployment has risen to unsustainably high levels. Service delivery at local government level is failing. Most provinces find themselves in a dire financial state and national government has borrowed almost to the hilt. Not one district in the Free State received a clean audit in 2019 nor did one of the 15 largest state-owned entities in the country. You can't fix it if you can't measure it.

As I write this, rebellions have welled up in Chile, a resource-rich, deeply unequal society much like South Africa. In Lebanon, too, people from all walks of life have taken to the streets in a highly organised protest movement. Following the events of the

Arab Spring which saw the overthrow of the likes of Mubarak in Egypt and Gaddafi in Libya, it is not unlikely that a similar scenario could play out here.

South Africa is a deeply challenging place in which to live and work – especially if you are poor, have little education and live in an under-serviced community. But it's in the very crisis in which South Africa finds itself today that there lies an enormous opportunity for renewal, growth and optimism.

Although this came to me third-hand and I cannot vouch for its provenance, the founder of an Israeli start-up is supposed to have told a recent gathering in Johannesburg: 'You can make a lot more money out of solving misery than you do out of providing comfort.'

It doesn't really matter who said it. If entrepreneurs in South Africa can find ways to alleviate the suffering of people who are otherwise helpless and unsupported, so as to make them productive members of society, then there is a better-than-even chance that the great democratic experiment begun more than 25 years ago in 1994 might just be fulfilled.

Because, if you want problems, you have come to the right place. South Africa is a land of crises. With pervasive inequality and too few opportunities for people to dig themselves out of the poverty trap into which they have been born, the country has the potential to sleepwalk into disaster. Business confidence is at multi-decade lows, the tax base is shrinking, migration is on the rise, and unless today's start-ups can be encouraged to grow and invest in this market, then the grim prognosis of many of the books on my shelf may just come to pass.

Yet it doesn't have to be that way.

At least part of the answer lies in the latest book on my shelf. It's by the Nobel Prize-winning economist Robert Shiller, called *Narrative Economics*, and it is all about how popular stories drive economic events. In a world of disinformation and internet trolls, where (certainly in the digital world) the loudest voices appear the most compelling, 'narrative economics' has extraordinary power. It can improve our ability to predict, prepare for, and mitigate the damage of financial crises, recessions, depressions and other economic disasters.

Ideas move markets. The Bank of England made it someone's job to monitor Donald Trump's Twitter feed after he became president because his musings did move markets. It doesn't matter whether they are true or not; if they gain traction, they have influence.

Shiller says the stories we tell ourselves about the world drive our behaviour, and if enough people buy into the same stories they will impact on the world at large. Stories influence the way we think and behave and, at scale, influence markets, affecting whether you invest or divest, and shaping your view on the long-term sustainability of a country.

Stories are critical.

Imagine if we told different stories.

In line with this kind of thinking, my book will tell you some of the stories of the extraordinary entrepreneurs who built globally competitive businesses in South Africa despite the upheaval, uncertainty and negativity prevailing at the time.

It will also introduce you to a new generation of courageous young people creating businesses that seek to solve the myriad problems South Africa faces today. These are the rebels, renegades and problem-solvers who, rather than allowing themselves to be caught up in the pervasive negativity, get stuck in to create solutions for the future.

They are considerably more useful to follow than the rascals, reprobates and problem-causers who litter the pages of most non-fiction titles about South Africa today. The latter do nothing for your sense of well-being and feelings of optimism for the future. Many of them should be in jail but are fighting tooth and nail to remain free so as to continue their career of looting and plunder.

There is a note just under the light switch in my children's music room at school. It reads:

Dear Optimists, Pessimists and Realists,
While you were arguing about the level of the water in the glass,
I drank it.
Regards
The Opportunist

Introduction

'The problem is not the problem. The problem is your attitude about the problem.' – Captain Jack Sparrow

It's hard to tell different stories when those in the mainstream are as dramatic and important as they are.

All hell broke loose at 8.08 pm on Wednesday, 9 December 2015. My radio producer, Cecile Basson, sent me an SMS: 'He's done it!'

'Who's done what?' I wondered as the Gautrain pulled out of Sandton Station en route to OR Tambo International Airport. Could it be her infant son taking his first steps?

In fact Jacob Zuma, the country's president, whom Max du Preez once dubbed a 'one-man wrecking ball', had done the unthinkable and fired his finance minister, Nhlanhla Nene. In doing so, he laid bare the state-capture project which so many in both the public and private sectors pretended did not exist. Very few people could have anticipated the economic devastation Zuma's action wrought in a relatively short period of time.

My mind started racing as I tried to process the implications of the decision and understand what would motivate a sitting president to make such an earth-shattering decision. With whom had he replaced Nene? Perhaps the situation wasn't so bad. Could he have seen sense and persuaded Trevor Manuel, the man who had restored the economic fortunes of South Africa from the ashes of apartheid, to return and restore global confidence in a rapidly failing state? It was possible but highly unlikely. Zuma and the no-nonsense Manuel were not likely collaborators in a project to procure a brighter future for the country.

A few bars of signal appeared at the top left of my cellphone screen. I tapped on my email app and there it was: a statement from the presidency.

'I have decided to remove Mr Nhlanhla Nene as Minister of Finance, ahead of his deployment to another strategic position,' read the statement. Nene had done nothing wrong, Zuma said. His skills were simply required elsewhere. He was being replaced not by his deputy, as was common practice in the National Treasury, but by a complete outsider, DDD van Rooyen.

A quick Google search showed that DDD van Rooyen, variously referred to by his first name of David and later by his common name, Des, was an ANC backbencher with no experience in government beyond a stint as a deeply unpopular mayor of Merafong City Municipality, a position from which he was publicly hounded by disgruntled residents who also burned his house down. This did not bode well.

By now I was at the airport and started making phone calls. Most numbers went to voicemail. One well-connected government official picked up the phone.

'What is he doing?' were the first words he uttered.

'I was hoping you would tell me,' I replied and we chatted briefly, speculating on the mystery redeployment and what we knew about Des van Rooyen. There wasn't much to say.

Unbeknown to us at the time, Nene had been summoned to a short meeting of no longer than three minutes with the president, at which he was informed that he was going to be shifted to a job at the newly formed BRICS bank – an offer that in the end failed to materialise.

Nene knew it was a ruse. Rumours of his imminent sacking had been circulating publicly for weeks. Indeed, Nene's deputy, Mcebisi Jonas, months before the axe fell, had warned his boss that his days at the helm of the Treasury were numbered and that he, Jonas himself, had been offered the job during a meeting at the now-infamous Gupta brothers' compound in Saxonwold. Jonas later said at the state-capture inquiry that he had met with Jacob Zuma's son Duduzane, businessman Fana Hlongwane and Ajay Gupta, one of the trio of brothers whose network infiltrated almost every level of government. They told him the job was his if he wanted it and, as a gesture of good faith, they would immediately give him R600,000 in cash, casually stuffed in wads into a black bin-bag, as a down payment to do their bidding were he to become finance minister. He was warned that if he revealed any details of the meeting, he would be killed.

Jonas, to his eternal credit, didn't bite. It was his refusal to buckle that led to the Van Rooyen appointment.

As I sat on the plane to Cape Town on the night the announcement of Nene's sacking was made, I became numb as I tried to come to terms with the magnitude of the problem the country faced. As the plane doors closed, I watched bond rates rocket on my market-tracking app and the currency sell-off begin. The world was panicking. The South African dream, it seemed, might well and truly be over.

As SA 375 thundered towards Cape Town, I wrote a column for EWN. The country was teetering on the edge of a precipice, but many people were going to bed that night blissfully unaware of the danger that South Africa was in.

'In elevating David [sic] van Rooyen, an ANC whip on the standing committee on finance, to arguably the most important job in the land, Zuma skipped Nene's deputy, the pragmatic and respected Mcebisi Jonas, as well as the next logical appointment, the chair of the standing committee on finance, Yunus Carrim – the former minister of communications – himself fired for doing too good a job in a dysfunctional ministry. This is Zuma's biggest gamble to date. It's a warning to the National Treasury, until now left to do the crucial work of balancing the country's books, that their refusal to fund nuclear builds, buy presidential aircraft or support the chair of SAA will get you fired.'

In the meantime, all hell was breaking loose at the National Treasury.

The director-general, Lungisa Fuzile, had been forewarned that trouble was coming. He'd received the heads-up from the chair of the ANC economic-transformation committee, Enoch Godongwana, who warned him that he was about to get a 'Gupta minister' who would arrive with his own advisers. It was clear that ANC members had joined the dots and were perfectly aware that the state-capture project was under way, but it was not until May 2017, when 200,000 emails discovered on a hard drive sent for repairs from the Guptas' private estate in Saxonwold were published, that the audacity and scale of the infiltration became apparent.

Van Rooyen reported for duty on the morning of 10 December, twelve hours after the announcement of his appointment was made, flanked by so-called advisers, to begin work.

During the night, bond markets had gone into serious decline and the value of the rand, already vulnerable amid low growth prospects and a failing state, had retreated sharply. Treasury officials had been fielding calls from all over the globe. Over the next two days R500bn would be wiped off the value of local markets. (Indeed since then, South Africa has been paying considerably more to borrow internationally than many of its developing-market peers, raising the interest component of the national budget, sucking money out of projects and work that could improve the lives of ordinary South Africans in terms of perpetually high interest rates.)

One of the new minister's advisers, Mohamed Bobat, who it would later emerge was the nephew of ANC deputy secretary-general, Jessie Duarte, started throwing his weight around. His actions, to those who observed them, seemed pretty deliberate. Duarte would later tell the *Mail & Guardian* that he had 'made mistakes'.

'He was not bothered that he was not an employee of the department and that his role had never been explained to me by anyone else other than himself,' Fuzile later told the Zondo Commission of Inquiry into state capture. 'Mr Bobat felt such a sense of authority and empowerment that he could issue instructions to anyone without first checking with [the incoming minister] on whose behalf he purported to act. He gave me the impression of being a law unto himself.'

It soon became clear to Fuzile that the new minister and his appointed adviser did not really know each other. It would later emerge that Bobat worked for a private-sector firm called Trillian, a financial-advisory company whose shareholders included a man called Salim Essa, who did business with the Gupta family and who was a shareholder with them in various ventures.

Bobat and the other adviser, Ian Whitley, wasted no time in leaking confidential Treasury documents to Trillian. Its CEO, Eric Wood, was already planning how he would take over various aspects of the department's work. Former ANC political heavyweight Tokyo Sexwale, who'd served as non-executive chairman of the company, quit spectacularly months later when a report by the respected advocate Geoff Budlender concluded that the company and its management could not be trusted. The blame game was well and truly under way.

Des van Rooyen would go on to serve about 94 hours as finance minister, the shortest term on record for a finance minister anywhere in the world. This seems typical of South Africa, which does nothing in half-measures: the country had previously broken the record for having the longest-serving finance minister in Trevor Manuel, who'd done a stint of more than 13 years. Van Rooyen became labelled the 'weekend special', after a popular song by the South African pop singer Brenda Fassie.

Unknown at the time was the sheer arrogance of the state-capture project, aided and abetted by local and multinational firms such as KPMG, SAP and Bain, as well as the crass manipulation of the public debate by the likes of London PR firm Bell Pottinger. The country was in such deep trouble that it was corroding from the inside as the cancer of corruption infiltrated everywhere. We have probably only just scratched the surface in learning exactly how bad it was allowed to become.

That fateful Friday night, 11 December, a group of friends gathered at the home of a well-known CEO for a long-scheduled house party. The mood was subdued. It was meant to be a festive end-of-year party – the kind you see in the movies where people drink too much and behave badly. But the mood at this gathering was less festive.

Talk was dominated by who had which passport, which assets could be quickly liquidated, and how money could be sent out of the country and what it would take to set up elsewhere. Precisely the kind of conversation that people of means have held at critical tipping points in South Africa's history.

Unbeknown to those at the party, high-level meetings had been happening for days. Every business leader with access to political players was delivering the same stern warning about the consequences of the president's actions. Key in those discussions was Patrice Motsepe, the lawyer turned billionaire businessman, who also had plenty to lose if South Africa failed. I asked him on the sidelines of a big corporate event in 2018 whether it was true that he'd sworn at Zuma out of sheer frustration on that extraordinary weekend. 'I did much worse than that,' he quipped, refusing to be drawn any further.

His intervention, sources say, was pivotal. Motsepe was a regular donor to Zuma and to causes linked to the president. In

October 2010, he committed himself to five annual donations to the president's foundation, which purported to help poor people with housing, education and clothing. The foundation rose to prominence in 2015 when images of its logo appeared at the garage of China's Formula E racing team, whose owner, Yu Liu, had business links to South Africa. The foundation's website made no mention of the sponsorship or the strategy behind it. The foundation's chair, Dudu Myeni, would later become the highly divisive chair at the national airline, SAA.

This closeness to Zuma enabled Motsepe to have a profound influence on the turn of events on that critical weekend. An intense meeting took place at the Union Buildings and led to Zuma backing down and returning Pravin Gordhan to the post of finance minister. And Van Rooyen, the hapless pawn, was shifted to the ministry of local government – a post from which he was removed when Cyril Ramaphosa later became president.

Back at the CEO's house, all those who'd come together for the house party went to bed early on Sunday in a sombre mood. No sooner had they retired to their rooms, after a feverish weekend of working out their plan-B exits from South Africa, than their host summoned them all back downstairs.

'He opened all the best wine he had,' a guest told me.

Sanity had prevailed. South Africa had pulled itself back from the brink.

'We can stay!' quipped one of the party. The rest toasted the sentiment.

Things were back to normal.

But what the hell is normal?

CHAPTER 1

How well do you know your country?

*'There's no room for facts when our minds are
occupied by fear.'* – Hans Rosling

We all have biases, whether we know them or not. Just how
fixed is your mindset when it comes to South Africa? Take this
quick quiz before we move on. Test members of your family. The
answers are on the pages that follow. (Don't cheat. I am watching
you.)

1. What was the inflation rate in 2004?
   (a) 18.7%
   (b) 4.7%
   (c) 1.4%

2. How many recessions have there been in South Africa since 1994?
   (a) 4
   (b) 3
   (c) 1

3. What percentage of South African households received a social
   grant in 2018?
   (a) 45%
   (b) 31%
   (c) 22%

4. Were more or fewer individuals in South Africa 'food secure' in
   2017 than in 2008?
   (a) More
   (b) Fewer
   (c) About the same

5. Male life expectancy in South Africa is on average …
   (a) 64.7 years
   (b) 61.5 years
   (c) 58.2 years

6. In South Africa, how many fatalities per 100,000 are there every
   year of children under the age of five?
   (a) 22.1
   (b) 28.5
   (c) 79

7. What percentage of families in South Africa live in informal homes?
   (a) 19%
   (b) 16%
   (c) 13%

8. What percentage of households use electricity for lighting?
    (a) 90.3%
    (b) 82.3%
    (c) 75.6%

9. What percentage of South African households have access to a
    flushing toilet?
    (a) 80%
    (b) 70%
    (c) 61%

10. What percentage of children aged 7–15 are enrolled in school?
    (a) 99%
    (b) 96%
    (c) 88%

11. What percentage of schools in South Africa have running water?
    (a) 86%
    (b) 74%
    (c) 69%

12. What percentage of South Africa's GDP comes from mining and
    agriculture?
    (a) 11%
    (b) 18%
    (c) 21%

13. How many murders are there every day in South Africa?
    (a) 67
    (b) 57
    (c) 47

14. How many ATMs are there in South Africa?
    (a) 29,500
    (b) 35,600
    (c) 37,900

15. How much bigger is GDP in dollar terms today than it was in 1994?
    (a) 2 times
    (b) 2.5 times
    (c) 3 times

16. R1,000 invested on the JSE in 1961, with dividends reinvested since then, is today worth …
    (a) R750,000
    (b) R7,500,000
    (c) R75,000,000

So, how did you do?

In his book *Factfulness* (2018), the late medical doctor and researcher Hans Rosling set about busting numerous myths we have about the world. The core purpose of his work was to restore perspective in a world that is moving and changing so fast with information flowing more quickly than ever before. It's very easy to get lost and, amid the deluge of information and the multiple political, social and economic agendas at play, start believing that the world (and, indeed for our purposes here, South Africa) is being sucked into a vortex of self-destruction.

Rosling observed through years of research that his audiences would routinely get basic questions about the state of the world wrong. When he asked them simple questions about global trends – such as: What percentage of the world's population lives in poverty? Why is the world's population increasing? How many girls finish school? – most would get the answers wrong.

Rosling and his family collaborators Anna and Ola asked why it is that our perspective of the world in which we live is distorted. We don't know what we don't know and therefore, when presented with a plausible explanation, we tend to accept it as fact on the basis of our cognitive biases, most of which are formed subconsciously.

Rosling deduced that despite the many imperfections in the world, it's in a far better shape than we might think. I would argue the same is true for South Africa. For all its deep flaws, it's actually in a better way than most of us think and certainly better than it was at any point in the apartheid era, despite many right-wing protestations to the contrary.

In a piece penned for the World Economic Forum in 2019, Discovery founder and CEO Adrian Gore explained the connection between optimism and evolutionary biology: 'With our earliest ancestors facing threats posed by violence, disease, child-birth and so on, the average lifespan was 21–35 years. To make any kind of progress in life, we needed to imagine a reality that was different, and one we believed was possible.'

The contradiction, he pointed out, is that we tend to balance personal optimism with 'declinism', in that we believe that the world and our country are persistently getting worse off and are in fact on an irreversible downhill trajectory.

Our worst fears are seldom realised, however. There are of course exceptions to every rule: Zimbabwe, Venezuela and Syria among them. Rosling doesn't seek to argue that bad things do not happen. He simply makes the point that most of the time our worst fears are not realised in the fullness of time. One works oneself up often, for no reason.

Rosling started the Gapminder Foundation in 2005 which he decided to use to counter ignorance with evidence. He set about challenging audience perceptions with questions about everyday life to reveal their cognitive biases. If you believe crime levels to be elevated in one area rather than another, hospital services there to be poor, and homelessness endemic, you will have a particular belief about how safe it is to venture into that area. What if data could show that all of these beliefs are false? You might have picked up on a social-media thread, got caught up in a particular WhatsApp group or simply been at a Sunday afternoon braai where opinions on a particular subject were being shared.

Consider images you see on the news about people living in squalor, and then being asked, as Rosling did of his subjects: 'In the past 20 years, the proportion of the world population living in extreme poverty has ...'

(a) Almost doubled
(b) Remained about the same
(c) Almost halved

Which did you choose?

Just 25% of respondents in wealthy Sweden and Norway got it right, and they were the most accurate among subjects from all countries surveyed.

Rosling doesn't disclose how South Africa voted. But it's likely that if you come from a poorer country, you will vote (a) or (b), when the correct answer is (c). When it comes to questions on basic health care and rates of vaccination, just 13% of respondents worldwide got the answers right. The more he tested people, the more Rosling found just how ignorant they were of basic facts.

'How could business people make sensible decisions for their organisations if their worldview was upside down? How could each person going about their life know which issues they should be stressed and worried about?' he wrote.

Rosling found humans tend to have an overly-dramatic worldview, and will often, with all the evidence in front of them, misinterpret facts. If things are bad right now, we assume they can only get worse. If there is lots of poverty, the assumption is that extreme poverty is on the rise.

'Step-by-step, year-by-year, the world is improving,' he wrote. 'Not on every single measure, every single year, but as a rule.'

Take the 2009 outbreak of swine flu. Modern technology and the 24-hour news cycle meant it was on TV all the time. Of course, the pandemic was serious. More than 200,000 people died. Contrast that with the Spanish flu of 1918 in which 2.7% of the world's population, mostly women, died. Over a two-week period, Rosling compared real data with public perceptions. During the time he observed cases of swine flu, 31 people died. Google searches threw up 253,443 articles about it, while more than 63,000 people died over the same period of TB. Each swine flu death had an average of 8,176 articles, in contrast to the TB issue, which had 0.1 articles per death. Swine flu thus received 82,000 times more attention.

TB is commonplace. It affects mostly poor people in poor communities. Swine flu could affect anyone, anywhere, at any time and, thanks to modern connectivity and air travel, could leapfrog around the globe in 24 hours. The news cycle reflected this and no doubt fuelled public fears on the issue. As this book is being edited, the Coronavirus is causing widespread panic as China goes into lockdown and countries develop strategies to deal with the outbreak of an illness that may or may not be contained.

Part of the problem, says Rosling, is that we are so overwhelmed by complex information, more so than in any preceding generation, that we like simple, linear ideas. We feel better about ourselves, more connected, more empowered if we can make sense of the world easily.

The world would be a much easier place to navigate if it were not so infernally complex. The notion of a free market, for example, is a simple idea, which presupposes that all government interference is bad and should be opposed at all costs. If equality is good, then inequality is the enemy; and if we redistributed a nation's entire resources for the greater good, our problems would disappear.

Would it not be wonderful if the world was so simple?

Our cognitive biases and desire for simplicity make us vulnerable to manipulation in a social-media age where, on the basis of our previous preferences, advertisers can target messaging to us that specifically confirms our view of the world, however misguided it may be. And if people who sell you washing powder and hamburgers can do it, so can people who want you to think a particular way politically. There is a growing body of research that suggests an increasing number of election outcomes may have been manipulated through data-driven, targeted advertising designed to plug into those biases.

Some 65% of people polled by Ipsos MORI in 28 countries told researchers they believed the world was getting worse, based precisely on the sorts of examples researched by Hans Rosling.

'We South Africans suffer from this declinist outlook acutely,' wrote Adrian Gore in 2019. 'Not only are South Africans gloomy about how the world has changed and what the future holds, on a broad range of issues, but South African respondents gave the least accurate guesses of where the figures on global and national development stood – out of all 28 countries. We are not just impervious to the facts on progress; the study revealed we are confident in our erroneous perceptions.'

So, let's get to the quiz I asked you to complete.

1. **What was the inflation rate in 2004?**
    (a) 18.7%
    (b) 4.7%
    (c) 1.4%
    Answer: (c) 1.4%

Unbelievable, isn't it? In the 1980s South Africa was grappling with double-digit inflation, peaking at 18.7% in 1986 following President PW Botha's disastrous Rubicon speech of 1985, which led to the effective collapse of the South African economy. In 1987 a young trade unionist called Cyril Ramaphosa led mine workers out on the biggest strike in the country's history, thereby adding to the crisis. That decade saw inflation average 14%. Money was losing half of its value every five years. It would have seemed inconceivable that in 2004 inflation would average 1.4%.

But it did. Most of the world endured higher inflation in the 1970s as a result of spikes in the oil price. As inflation calmed in South Africa's biggest trading partners, it eased locally too. Currency weakness is also a key driver of inflation in South Africa, which often runs big trade deficits as we consume more than we make as a country. Government introduced inflation targeting with a range of 3%–6% in the 2000/1 budget to forestall the possibility of the kind of crises that had enveloped the country in previous decades. And it worked. The world moved into a period of low inflation and, after the currency shocks of the late 1990s and early 2000s, the rand started to strengthen again, thereby limiting the impact of import inflation. The cost of electronics, in particular, plummeted and more South Africans than ever before were able to afford white household goods, cellphones and other electronic devices. Low inflation is good for growth, and between 2004 and 2007 South Africa recorded its highest growth rate since the 1960s, averaging 5.2% per annum. Jobs were created and the country felt unbeatable.

2. **How many recessions have there been in South Africa since 1994?**

    (a) 4

    (b) 3

    (c) 1

    Answer: (c) 1

It depends, of course, on how you define 'recession'. A recession really is a full-year contraction in growth, but we make the distinction in South Africa between recession and technical recession, the latter being defined as two consecutive quarters of economic contraction. We have had one year where growth fell below zero and that was 2009, when the economy shrank by 1.5%. But thanks to the hustle and bustle of preparations for the 2010 Soccer World Cup and the building boom that accompanied it, there was a quick recovery to above 3% a year. Since 2014, however, the economy has not managed to grow by more than 2%, and there have been several serious slowdowns. The most serious was in 2018 when Cyril Ramaphosa ousted Jacob Zuma as president. After a brief period of expansion thanks to the effects of Ramaphoria, reality set in and the country experienced a technical recession.

But the country's luck ran out in 2019 when Eskom introduced Stage 6 load-shedding for the first time, ironically on 9 December 2019, the fourth anniversary of the sacking of Nhlanhla Nene. This was Cyril Ramaphosa's 9/12. Eskom instructed its mining-industry clients to cease all but the most essential work until it could stabilise the power grid, and the country descended into a deep funk.

Previously, government had blamed the global financial crisis and its aftermath for its own failure to inject confidence into a failing state. The 2008 recession was due to a global loss of confidence in markets, but the rest of the world moved swiftly on thereafter as a result of pragmatic and reliable reforms. South Africa stuttered along, incapable of providing the very basic commodity a 21st-century economy needs to flourish – energy. In January 2020, however, new Eskom CEO André de Ruyter hit the ground running. The former head of Sasol coal has quickly managed to get a firm grip on the realities of the operational issues and, while South Africans might not appreciate his diagnosis and proposed remedies, there is a chance that the country's biggest liability will now be professionally managed.

By contrast, in the two decades preceding the 1994 democratic elections there were seven periods of full-blown recession, the worst of which was an almost-unbroken period of economic decline between 1990 and 1993. The ANC has been a very effective steward of the South African economy, but without significant policy reforms, the odds of returning to the +5% heydays of 2004–8 are remote.

If you take economist Dawie Roodt's definition of recession as being economic growth underperforming population growth, then South Africa has been in an almost-unbroken state of recession for the past five years. When population growth outstrips economic growth, on average the population gets poorer, and that has been the curse of economic policy mismanagement in recent years.

South Africa's unemployment trend is a national crisis, and

without swift, meaningful policy reforms designed to encourage growth, the declines will persist.

3. **What percentage of South African households received a social grant in 2018?**
   (a) 45%
   (b) 31%
   (c) 22%
   Answer: (b) 31%

Ironically, one of our government's greatest achievements, that of a social wage for those who cannot work or find employment, is also an admission of failure: a failure to create a growth-supporting economic environment that would deliver jobs and increase revenue for projects that would further reduce unemployment. Each year, National Treasury budgets for an increase in social grants. If only the social-grant bill could be reduced because people didn't need it. South Africa budgeted an astonishing R567bn for social grants in 2019.

A total of 44.3% of households in South Africa receive at least one social grant, up from 30.8% in 2003. The highest proportion of households dependent on grants is in the Eastern Cape, where 59% of households receive some form of state support, closely followed by the Northern Cape at 57.4% and the Free State at 50.7%. Depending on where you live, there are more or fewer work opportunities, a situation that affects your dependence on the state. In sharp contrast to the Eastern Cape, grant payments are least prevalent in Gauteng and the Western Cape, where there are greater levels of economic opportunity. In Gauteng 30% of households received at least one grant, and in the Western Cape 36.7%.

Stats SA figures also reflect South Africa's legacy of racial polarisation. More than one in three black South Africans depend on a grant, compared to 29.9% of so-called coloured people, and 12.5% of Indians. This is in stark contrast to the 7.5% of white South Africans reliant on the state.

For every R1,000 government spent in 2016/17, R14 went to social protection. Social grants have been successful in reducing extreme poverty. According to the United Nations *Sustainable Development Goals Report 2019*, social grants had reduced the poverty headcount rate by 7.9% and the poverty gap by 29.5%.

Grants are the second most important source of income for South African households after salaries, according to Stats SA's *General Household Survey 2018*.

4. **Were more or fewer individuals in South Africa 'food secure' in 2017 than in 2008?**
    (a) More
    (b) Fewer
    (c) About the same
    Answer: (a) More

The right to food is enshrined in the South African constitution, and, according to the 2018 Global Food Security Index, South Africa is ranked as the most food-secure country in Africa and 45th out of 133 countries worldwide.

But, observed the communications officer for the NGO Grow Great, Ofentse Mboweni, in the *Mail & Guardian* of 15 October 2019, South Africa has a disproportionately high rate of stunting due to malnutrition, particularly among children under five, relative to other African countries. 'South Africa's prevalence of stunting is far higher than one would expect for a country that ranks as the most food-secure country on the continent; it is much higher than its development counterparts Gabon, Ghana and Senegal, which rank lower than South Africa on the Global Food Security Index,' Mboweni wrote. 'National dietary surveys estimate that 77% of children between the ages of six and 23 months do not receive a minimally acceptable diet and that 2.5 million children live below the food poverty line, because there is insufficient money in their households to cover the cost of their basic nutritional needs.'

This is further borne out by NGOs that work in the education sector, which report dramatic improvements in outcomes by students when even rudimentary nutrition programmes are introduced in schools in impoverished areas.

Food security in South Africa has, however, increased in leaps and bounds, showing a 50% improvement between 2005 and 2008. There has also been a marked improvement in the number of households that are deemed vulnerable to hunger, from 24.2% in 2002 to 10.4% in 2017.

5.   Male life expectancy in South Africa is on average ...
    (a) 64.7 years
    (b) 61.5 years
    (c) 58.2 years
    Answer: (b) 61.5 years

The figure is low by global standards but improving. A boy born in South Africa today can expect to live an average of 61.5 years;

a girl, 67.7 years. The average life expectancy of a South African in 2002 was 55, but that increased to 65 in 2019. The numbers were skewed by a spike in mortality rates between 2002 and 2006 largely as a result of the HIV and AIDS pandemic and the failure of the Thabo Mbeki government to address the crisis properly. If there was one significant achievement of the Zuma years, it was to dispense with the Mbeki-era obsession with beetroot and African potato diets, and to introduce large-scale antiretroviral programmes, as a result of which life expectancy is increasing. So too is the potential for someone who carries the virus to lead a productive life and make a positive contribution to society.

6. **In South Africa, how many fatalities per 100,000 are there every year of children under the age of five?**
    (a) 22.1
    (b) 28.5
    (c) 79
    Answer: (b) 28.5

Infant mortality rates have more than halved in South Africa between 2002 and 2019, from an estimated 56.5 deaths per 1,000 live births 18 years ago to 22.1 in 2019. The mortality rate for children under five years of age has also declined markedly: this is attributable to the better distribution of antiretrovirals and the fact that households have better access to food thanks in no small part to social grants. In 2002, some 79 children out of every 1,000 died before the age of five. That number is now down to 28.5 – a remarkable achievement, though the figure is significantly higher than more developed economies, such as Sweden at 2.8 and the

UK at 4.9. Singapore has the best track record in terms of getting children to survive past their fifth birthday: only 2.3 children per 1,000 don't make it past that landmark age in the city-state.

7. **What percentage of families in South Africa live in informal homes?**
    (a) 19%
    (b) 16%
    (c) 13%
    Answer: (c) 13%

According to Stats SA's Community Survey 2016, the percentage of households living in formal dwellings increased from 65% in 1996 to 79% in 2016, while those classed as living in a 'traditional dwelling' fell from 18.3% to 7% over the same period. This suggests that many people from rural areas living in the cities have invested in building family homes in the villages they come from – and there is plenty of evidence for this in the results of businesses like Cashbuild and other building suppliers. Not enough has been done, though, to alleviate the burden on people who live in informal homes. That number has grown in real terms from 1.4 million dwellings in the 1996 census, to nearly 2.2 million structures today. As a percentage of homes occupied, however, the ratio has been reduced from 16% to 13% over the same period.

8. **What percentage of households use electricity for lighting?**
    (a) 90.3%
    (b) 82.3%
    (c) 75.6%
    Answer: (a) 90.3%

While South Africa is chronically short of reliable electricity, thanks to catastrophic policy failings, poor management and large-scale fraud at the state-owned power monopoly Eskom, when there is electricity more than 90% of homes are lit by an electric bulb. The percentage of households using electricity for lighting increased from 58.1% in 1996 to 90.3% in 2016. Eskom has a huge problem on its hands because it is unable to collect from certain municipalities. President Cyril Ramaphosa in October 2019 pleaded with residents of Soweto in particular to end the culture of non-payment which helped bankrupt the apartheid state, but which is now at risk of doing the same thing to the country post-liberation.

The township's R1.3bn electricity bill was written off in 2003 when it was amalgamated with the City of Johannesburg municipality, and around the same time Eskom took over billing responsibility for Soweto. That seems to be where it all started going wrong on an industrial scale. Government claims Eskom is owed R18bn overall by delinquent municipalities, though local rights groups dispute this. Whatever the number, until Eskom can bill individual properties, it will be stuck in a position where it may have to embark on mass shut-offs that will anger entire communities, particularly those that do pay their way.

9. **What percentage of South African households have access to a flushing toilet?**
    (a) 80%
    (b) 70%
    (c) 61%
    Answer: (c) 61%

In addition to electrification, there have been other developments in raising health levels and giving citizens a more dignified life, and while progress is slow, it's useful to note that there are twice as many households in South Africa today than there were in 1996.

So while just 60.6% of households have access to a flushing toilet today compared to 49.1% of those surveyed in 2001, the real number is considerably higher than the ratio suggests. But still four out of ten households do not have proper sanitation – a worldwide phenomenon in poorer countries, for which organisations such as the Bill and Melinda Gates Foundation are trying to find solutions, by allocating massive grants to scientists to discover better ways of disposing of human waste.

While far from ideal, the number of households whose refuse is removed once a week has improved from 52% in 1996 to 60.1% in 2016. This largely explains why poor areas are left to wallow in mountains of rubbish, and wealthier areas not. If you can't get your rubbish removed and taken to a central disposal point, it finds its way onto the streets and ultimately into waterways, just like much of the raw sewage that flows into river systems, many of which deliver your drinking water.

10. **What percentage of children aged 7–15 are enrolled in school?**
    (a) 99%
    (b) 96%
    (c) 88%
    Answer: (a) 99%

Let's be clear: 'enrolled' is not the same as 'attending' or 'engaging' or even 'muddling through'. According to government statistics, just 51% of children aged 7–15 were enrolled in school in 1994, whereas that number had increased by 2018 to 99%. Access to primary health care during that time also improved, according to the Department of Health's statistics. When measured in terms of visits to health-care facilities, there were 67 million in 1998 and the number increased to 128 million by March 2018. While the improvements are admirable, what is not measured is outcomes. Although infant- and child-mortality statistics suggest a marked improvement in health care, the same cannot be said for education. According to the 2016 Progress in International Reading Literacy Study (PIRLS), 78% of Grade 4s cannot read for meaning in any language in this country. More on this critical issue later.

11. **What percentage of schools in South Africa have running water?**
    (a) 86%
    (b) 74%
    (c) 69%
    Answer: (b) 74%

According to education researcher Nic Spaull, more than a quarter of South Africa's schools do not have access to running water, and this explains why so many still have pit toilets. The issue has been brought to public attention in a series of harrowing stories reported by pressure groups like Section 29. These have exposed the failure of the education department to create decent conditions in which children can learn. In 2019 the minister of basic education, Angie Motshekga, pledged to rid schools of pit toilets 'within three years' – and the clock is ticking. It's hard to see how she will achieve that goal, considering the fact that many of the schools which have pit latrines (some 3,898 of those in all) are situated in areas where there is no available piped water and where there are no formal sewerage facilities either. The problem is far bigger than the schools themselves. It will require new technologies rather than the hope that flushing systems will be introduced.

12. **What percentage of South Africa's GDP comes from mining and agriculture?**
    (a) 11%
    (b) 18%
    (c) 21%
    Answer: (a) 11%

Considering the amount of airtime mining gets in terms of jobs and labour relations, you might be forgiven for thinking the number was bigger than it actually is. Gold mining in South Africa is all but dead. Gold Fields operates just one mine in South Africa, at South Deep, and at the time of writing, AngloGold Ashanti is in the process of selling off its last mine to focus on more profitable projects elsewhere, while the once-mighty DRDGold now concentrates on extracting gold from tailings dumped a hundred years ago by using better technologies than their forebears. It's hard to believe that on the day Nelson Mandela was released from prison in 1990, 23 of the top 40 companies listed on the JSE were gold miners. But reserves have become depleted, and a mix of safety concerns and rising costs means that even South African miners with an appetite for risk, operating at the deepest levels of any mines in the world, 4 kilometres below the surface, are calling it a day.

Agriculture, like mining, has been plagued by policy uncertainty in recent years. South African mining became all but uninvestible in the dying days of the Zuma administration when Mosebenzi Zwane (of Estina Dairy project fame) was launched into the mining department and, as minister, oversaw the creation of a charter that threatened to scupper for good the industry upon which the country's wealth was built.

Agriculture also has had a rough ride, with potentially more trouble ahead, depending on how the current land debate pans out. More and more farms are held in fewer and fewer hands as large-scale mechanisation has led to a decrease in farmers and a massive increase in the amount of land those that still run them can harvest. While agriculture contributes just 2% directly to GDP, it does provide about 700,000 jobs, down from decades ago, but it remains an important employer. There are believed to be about 35,000 white commercial farmers in South Africa and about 5,000 black farmers – the latter number is steadily growing. While individual farmers may be farming more land, the size of the properties remains largely unaltered. Just 0.2% of farms in South Africa are larger than 12,000 hectares, and many of these encompass less attractive soil types in drier areas such as the Karoo.

Farming and mining, once regarded as the mainstays of the South African economy, are far less relevant today than they were thirty-odd years ago. Manufacturing and construction, though both under pressure, have grown to about 20% of GDP while the vast majority of economic activity comes from the services sector, a trend which is reflected in the vastly changed make-up of the Top 40 shares on the JSE compared to those in 1990.

13.   **How many murders are there every day in South Africa?**
     (a) 67
     (b) 57
     (c) 47
     Answer: (b) 57

It's a terrifying statistic. Nearly 21,000 South Africans who have already survived the lottery of making it past their fifth birthday in one piece meet their end at the hands of someone else each year. Most murders happen at the weekend. Some 70% of killings occur between 9 pm on a Friday and 3 am the following Monday.

Police classify murders in three broad categories:
- criminal behaviour, or murders that happen as a result of other crimes and criminal activity;
- group behaviour, where gangs murder each other, taxi violence erupts, or mobs seek out vigilante justice; and
- antisocial behaviour, such as alcohol and drug abuse, dysfunctional relationships, unemployment and other social problems leading to deaths.

The Western Cape is home to a third of the country's 30 most murderous areas, with Nyanga the most dangerous place in South Africa, and six out of the top ten most violent policing areas are in the province. Despite its fearsome reputation, Johannesburg Central was ranked 17th overall. Just 3% of police stations in the country's most violent areas accounted for 21% of all killings.

According to the Institute for Security Studies, there were 66.9 murders per 100,000 people in 1994, and that number has fallen to around 32 today. The murder rate, even though the threat of violence feels ever present, has in fact halved in South Africa over the past quarter of a century.

14. How many ATMs are there in South Africa?
    (a) 29,500
    (b) 35,600
    (c) 37,900
    Answer: (c) 37,900

South Africa has boxed above its weight from a fintech perspective over recent decades. As the country still has a high level of dependency on cash for transactions, it follows that we should have a high number of ATMs (the first was tried out at the Rand Easter Show in 1981). The digital revolution is taking hold with the creation of a new generation of digital-only banks and the inevitable shuttering and scaling down of bank branches which are no longer needed as in the days of queues and bank tellers.

15. How much bigger is GDP in dollar terms today than it was in 1994?
    (a) 2 times
    (b) 2.5 times
    (c) 3 times
    Answer: (b) 2.5 times

And it could have been so much bigger had it not been for the virtual stagnation of the second Zuma administration, during which there was widespread corruption and much government spending which should have been directed to uplifting the poor but ended up being ferreted away by a wide range of criminal activities. While South Africa has seen a devaluation of its currency, the economy in dollar terms is more than twice the size it was in 1994, thanks largely to the massive expansion of corporates not only in South Africa but also beyond its borders. South African pension funds are home to 82% of Africa's retirement savings, while the country has spawned a host of globally competitive businesses that have at various points in time become significant players in new markets. Most notable was SABMiller, which has now been subsumed largely into Anheuser-Busch InBev, while firms like Growthpoint, Billiton, Anglo and Bidcorp among others have shown an ability to stand their ground in a tough global environment.

16. R1,000 invested on the JSE in 1961, with dividends reinvested since then, is today worth …
   (a) R750,000
   (b) R7,500,000
   (c) R75,000,000
   Answer: Seriously? You want everything for nothing, don't you? For this answer you are going to have to do some work. The answer is tucked away elsewhere in the book.

You cannot argue that South Africa is worse off today than it was in 1994. Nelson Mandela inherited a bankrupt state, economically, politically and morally, and set about creating an environment in which confidence drove growth. While key indicators such as consumer confidence and business confidence are now at decades-worst lows, there is a new vibrancy emerging among a new generation of entrepreneurial problem-solvers eager to tackle the nation's problems as opportunities so as to rebuild a country that has been involved in the equivalent of 15 rounds with Muhammad Ali in the famous Rumble in the Jungle. South Africa is bruised and battered. Its sense of self-confidence is low, as it sits for the first time in our modern democracy on the brink of a downgrade to sub-investment grade.

The Zuma decade did considerable damage to the country, and Cyril Ramaphosa arguably has a tougher job than Nelson Mandela did in 1994, when there was a sense of optimism and hope, which eludes the country today. If we'd just carried on at 3%–4% growth over the past decade, we might have halved poverty and created as many as 2.5 million jobs. No wonder we are despondent.

But South Africa is a place where remarkable things are happening, and as former FNB CEO Michael Jordaan puts it: 'Confidence is the cheapest form of stimulus you can get.'

So that raises the question: How do we acquire some of that confidence? Perhaps we should start by looking at the facts of our country, rather than the extraordinary distortions we are fed daily. We need growth. Without it, jobs don't happen. Without jobs and a reason to get up in the morning, families cannot prosper. Hope dies.

So instead of looking at problems, the focus should be on fixing them. The country needs a vision it can take seriously. You cannot tell people who now are never sure when they board a Metrorail train whether they will still have their cellphone at the end of the journey, or will even get to work on time, that they can dream of a future of smart cities and bullet trains. Their present reality is just too stark to contemplate such a future. We need to take small, deliberate, incremental steps that lead as quickly as possible to more opportunities for more people.

We need to acknowledge and build on our successes and tackle the problems with an appropriate level of skills necessary for fixing them. We cannot go to the world and ask it to fulfil President Cyril Ramaphosa's lofty ambition of $100bn in foreign direct investment if South Africans themselves are offshoring their wealth faster than you can say 'briefcase across the border'. Recognising the potential of our economy and investing in it, says Discovery's Adrian Gore, is the way change happens.

As he says, 'Attitude drives fundamentals, not the other way around.'

CHAPTER 2

An extraordinary series of incredible events

*'Logic will get you from A to B. Imagination will
take you everywhere.'* – Albert Einstein

Not long after Nhlanhla Nene was fired in December 2015, I was
in a pub in Manchester in England. Instead of bemoaning the fate
of my homeland, I was instead marvelling at the high number
of beers on sale at the bar that had been brewed by SABMiller,
which was in the throes of a takeover by private-equity-funded
AB InBev. Sitting alongside local brands Tetley and Boddingtons,
they were all there: Grolsch, Foster's, Peroni, Pilsner Urquell,
Tyskie …

SAB had been a very successful virtual monopoly, brewing
Castle Lager, Lion Lager, Ohlsson's, Hansa and Black Label for
the South African market. For domestic consumers, choice was
a foreign idea. Provided the beer was plentiful, cold and frothy,
South African drinkers were not particularly discerning.

SAB's greatest strength was that despite its domestic dominance, it had never allowed itself to be complacent. It had

fine-tuned its processes and used its leading position to perfect its brewing of massive volumes of beer cost-effectively, marketing its product, and finding the best way of getting it to consumers. It created a highly efficient production process with a world-class marketing machine to ensure its customers kept coming back for more.

Those lessons would stand it in good stead when it entered new markets after 1990. With the end of apartheid coinciding with the fall of the Berlin Wall, the world opened up to South African companies, which had been restricted until that time from global expansion.

Unlike many later South African companies that moved beyond their traditional market, SAB didn't fly headlong into big, expensive deals. It built up its understanding of different markets by proceeding cautiously at first, moving through numerous African countries and buying up breweries that produced well-loved local brands before arriving in Eastern Europe, where it was able to quickly refresh brands that had been neglected for decades.

There developed a race for global domination as other ambitious brewers looked to seize the Eastern Europe opportunity too. SAB listed in London to raise capital for big expansions and moved into the US with its acquisition of Miller and then over the following years bought strong brands across the globe.

For a while it became the biggest brewer in the world. That was until Anheuser-Busch bought Belgium's InBev to create AB InBev. It would eventually swallow SABMiller, but not before shareholders had squeezed every cent of the $102bn out of the private-equity players for the then London-listed company. Billed at that time as the biggest-ever corporate takeover in UK history, the deal created a truly global player with operations in almost every market on earth. Shareholders did not let go easily, and it turns out they could not have timed their exit better.

Global liquor-consumption data shows that beer drinking worldwide peaked in 2007 and has been steadily decreasing since then. Other beverages have been eroding market share, particularly in the core male beer-drinking market. The spirits industry has boxed smart and produced cool, easily accessible beverages in the ready-to-drink category. Firms like Bermuda-based Bacardi, France's Pernod Ricard and Japan's Suntory have created new-generation products that have appealed to growing disposable-income levels in wealthier economies. All this has come at the expense of beer. Fruit-flavoured, vodka-based drinks have taken the lion's share of this new drinking market.

This development has forced other categories to innovate and they have adapted faster than beer. New trends show that consumers are prepared to drink sparkling wine out of a can through a straw, provided the product is properly marketed. Brewers have been slow to respond to the rapidly evolving environment and have struggled to stay relevant.

But a growing number of brands are positioning themselves as lower-calorie, healthier options as tastes and trends change. It's proving a problem now for AB InBev, which is by far the biggest producer of a drink whose popularity is decreasing.

SABMiller shareholders cashed in, just in time. Before the AB InBev offer, shares in the world's second-biggest brewer had been trading at £29.34. AB InBev offered £40 per share, but SABMiller refused. There was a break fee of $3bn – the amount AB InBev would need to pay if it walked away from the deal. The price gradually ratcheted up. £42.15 was rejected, as was £43.50. It felt for a while that SABMiller might push just a little too hard. Finally the parties settled on £44 per share – a 50% premium on the ruling price before the offer was made. For the little brewer from number 2 Jan Smuts Avenue, Johannesburg, it was a triumph. No other South African company had seen its shareholders rewarded so handsomely.

But none of this happened by accident.

Heritage was critical to the SAB story. It traced its roots back to a man called Charles Glass whose supposed signature still adorns every bottle of the modern-day brew. Glass brewed Castle Beer in the early mining days of Johannesburg. He started in 1886, the same year that Johannesburg was founded amid the chaos of the mining claims that had been staked on the Witwatersrand following the discovery of rich gold-bearing reef by the prospector George Harrison. The Castle brewery would become the first non-mining share listed on the fledgling JSE two years later. It would also list on the London Stock Exchange until the 1960s when political pressure forced it to move its primary listing to the JSE.

By 1999 South Africa had just elected its second democratic government and executive teams at the big corporations were under pressure to grow internationally. Some did so more successfully than others. SAB was one of a handful that did well. It created a new UK-based holding company, SAB plc, and moved its primary listing back to London.

Three years later it had mustered the firepower to buy rival Miller Brewing, maker of Budweiser's biggest domestic rival beers. It followed this in 2005 by taking a major interest in Bavaria SA, the second-biggest brewer in South America. Miller proved a tough nut to crack and in 2008, just as the global financial crisis was looming, it teamed up with Molson Coors and created a beverages joint venture to stand against the might of Anheuser-Busch in that market.

Its battle for Foster's turned hostile, until the Australian board finally capitulated in a $10bn deal. SABMiller got everything except the rights to sell the Australian beer in Europe and the UK. In the complex world of brewing, these rights were owned by Heineken, a family-controlled brewer that would successfully stave off SABMiller's advances in 2014, leaving the firm that had started out in Joburg 128 years before vulnerable to takeover itself. By the time the AB InBev acquisition was concluded in October 2016, SABMiller was present in 80 countries and had the proud title of providing the world's biggest beer by volume, China's Snow beer, in addition to brands like Grolsch, Pilsner Urquell and Foster's.

With all of this racing through my mind as I sipped my beer in the Manchester pub, I marvelled at the ingenuity of the underdog from the emerging market who'd taken on the world's best and won – at least until that point. Maybe, considering the price SABMiller shareholders received for their stock, they still are the winners.

As I left the pub, contemplating the extraordinary success

of SABMiller, a small white truck emerged from the gathering gloom of the mid-afternoon Manc dusk. It was an extraordinary moment. I blinked twice, remembered that I'd had just one pint of local bitter and so was unlikely to be hallucinating, but the little white truck really did have a Bidvest food services logo on the side. Bidvest would later unbundle its large global food-services operation to create Bidcorp and leave its core industrial-services businesses on the JSE.

Unlike many failed South African ventures abroad, Bidvest founder and then CEO Brian Joffe had brought quality companies into the fold and did not waste time on having to fix broken goods. The company is likely to flourish globally, detached from the apron strings of the Johannesburg home base, and has operations practically everywhere except in the cut-throat US environment. Time will tell if it can muster up the courage to enter that enormous market.

'What are the odds of that?' I mused. Fancy eyeing all these South African-connected beers in a single pub only to emerge to see a Bidvest-branded truck go by.

And then I saw the Nando's logo as the Bidvest truck slowly made its way through the afternoon traffic. Had I been in London that day and a smartly dressed financial adviser had stopped me and offered to sell me life assurance provided by Old Mutual, or if a Santam broker offered me short-term cover, or an Investec banker offered me an account, I would probably have bought it. Such was the level of patriotism in me at that moment.

Many South African companies were then boxing above their weight and performing well in foreign markets. Tragically, the lessons learned were neither universal nor were they transferred to new generations of managers.

Hundreds of billions of rand would be spent on global expansion by South African companies. No one knows precisely how much: neither the Reserve Bank, nor the National Treasury, nor, despite my best efforts, the investment industry, nor academia. Perhaps it's an impossible task.

Later on, I will share with you some of the more spectacular South African investment catastrophes, primarily among retailers. But the big guys weighed in too. In March 2010 I wrote a cover story for *Finweek* magazine about Old Mutual's failing R100bn global acquisition spree that followed its unbundling at the end of the 1990s and its listing on the London Stock Exchange in 1999. The group became too big and unwieldy – at one point it owned 50 companies in 35 jurisdictions – bolting on acquisitions left, right and centre, doing complex mergers that simply didn't work, and destroying shareholder value in the process. Ironically, throughout its global gallivanting, the domestic market remained the company's biggest earner and remained so until its unbundling and return to a primary listing on the JSE in 2018.

As I said in that *Finweek* story: 'its South African operations, maligned internationally for their perceived political and currency risk, have been the cash cow for the group's failed international expansion ... Old Mutual's track record stands as a monument to flawed decision-making. In retrospect, its helter-skelter globalisation lacked effective oversight. Some of that may be down to the fact that then CEO and chairman Mike Levett held both positions on the board and relinquished the latter only in 2005 when Old Mutual acquired Skandia. It was during Levett's tenure as chairman that its poor acquisitions were made: in 2000 it bought Gerrard Private Bank for more than R5bn and proceeded to merge several existing British businesses with it – only to sell the enlarged business in 2003 to Barclays plc for less than half of what it paid. In the two years following Old Mutual's acquisition of United Asset Management (UAM) in 2000 for more than R15bn, markets went into decline: the Standard & Poor's 500 shed 12% in 2001 and a further 20% the next year, affecting not only profits but also its level of assets under management. It was during this period that the group announced the acquisition of Fidelity and Guaranty Life for R4bn. In 2008 Old Mutual recapitalised it to the tune of R16bn.'

There was a lot more, but I am sure you get the picture. While not all South African companies covered themselves in glory globally, some did. I will tell you some of those stories.

CHAPTER 3

Opportunity knocks

'Negative people never build anything.' – Piet Mouton

Ever since Jan van Riebeeck set up a refreshment station on behalf of the Dutch East India Company at the Cape of Good Hope in 1652, South Africa has proved to be a treasure trove for opportunists seeking to make a buck – the faster the better.

Long before the Nkandla scandal broke – long before South Africans discovered their president allowed R249m of taxpayers' money to be used to fund his now-crumbling private rural estate in KZN – the governor of the Cape did something remarkably similar. Willem Adriaan van der Stel, who is remembered with far less affection than his industrious father Simon, after whom both Simonstown and Stellenbosch are named, exploited a loophole in colonial governance for considerable personal gain. He was the forerunner of so many since who, once they have acceded to power, believe the rules no longer apply to them, and that they will never be held to account for their transgressions.

In the early 1700s it took months for communications from the Cape to reach Holland and vice versa. This made it possible to get up to all kinds of mischief in the certain knowledge that if word did ever reach HQ, it would be many months before there would be any threat of retribution or consequence for one's actions. You could string out all kinds of malfeasance for years. It turns out that even in the digital age, 21st-century transgressors have been able to do precisely the same thing.

Willem Adriaan van der Stel must have figured that if he moved quickly, he would be able to cement his position as a leading member of the landed gentry at the Cape without interference. At the same time, his vision of free enterprise was built on the back of slavery and the fact that colonists had a captive market. There was nowhere within a three-month voyage of the Cape that provided the same level of shelter, safety and access to fresh produce as the Cape. Sea journeys in the days before refrigeration were arduous, and the existence of the refreshment station, now a rapidly growing town at the foot of Table Mountain, enabled the trade in spices, silks and humanity to proceed almost unhindered.

The governor not only did not want to miss out on the action but also sought to capitalise on it while the going was good, and he set about creating an extraordinary estate on the banks of the Lourens River. The property, named Vergelegen, literally 'situated far away', was about as remote as you could be in those days while still having access to the market that Cape Town provided. The centre of government at the Castle was sufficiently distant yet the town retained its allure for market opportunities.

Van der Stel built his own African Versailles on the Lourens River and, according to the historian Professor Leo Fouché, created a 'palatial' Vergelegen – a 'monument to magnificence'. That monument to excess would be his downfall. He incurred the wrath of the burghers of the Cape, led by Adam Tas, who would spend time incarcerated in the dungeon at the Castle for his trouble. But the burghers submitted their complaints to the Heren XVII, the Amsterdam-based council of the Dutch East India Company, and after what appears to have been years of back-and-forth correspondence, they recalled their man. Van der Stel junior would eventually die in poverty, disgrace and obscurity in Holland.

The original manor house on the farm, now owned by Anglo American, was rebuilt years later. The majestic 350-year-old camphor trees standing in front of the house, imported as seedlings from Java, are national monuments by virtue of the fact that they are the oldest-known cultivated trees in the country. The property remains as a monument to extravagance and a reminder that eventually the truth prevails and justice is served.

Willem Adriaan van der Stel's story has been repeated many times over in a country that has been a honeypot for opportunists over the centuries. Many of them have operated with gay abandon and with no thought of the consequences of their actions. Fortunately there have been those who have spotted opportunities that have created legitimate enterprises and have in turn helped build the continent's most powerful economy.

After the original settlement at the Cape, the first real rush in the colonial era for a fast buck came with the discovery of diamonds at Kimberley, followed some 20 years later by the discovery of gold on the Witwatersrand, which would see a mad stampede of fortune-seekers flooding into the country. Long before apartheid had a name, it had a form, and black South Africans' opportunity to capitalise on the discovery of minerals was soon confined to that of labourers.

The South African economy in the 19th and 20th centuries was built on mining and on commercial agriculture. It was only after 1994, as South Africa became part of a global economy, that diversification occurred on a grand scale and the economy became more inclusive and diverse, but it was those with economic and educational advantage who were best positioned to capitalise on the financial opportunities that political freedom brought in 1994. Prior to democracy, the exclusion of black South Africans, always the vast majority of the population, from the economic mainstream had created a massive drag on progress. Indeed, rather than fulfilling the nationalist ambition of empowering Afrikaners, apartheid held back not only the development of a nation, but also that of the very people in whose name it was devised and executed.

It is nothing if not ironic that the fall of apartheid brought greater economic liberation to more Afrikaners than the National Party ever did. While the fall of apartheid and the Afrikaner nationalist state gave black South Africans their political freedom, it also forced Afrikaners to rethink their future without the sheltering protection of the state. Armed with skills, capital and the realisation that they had nowhere else to go, many seized the economic opportunity that political liberation brought.

As the legendary *Sunday Times* editor Ken Owen observed in 1994, following the ANC's ascent to power, it was now the turn of the Afrikaners to make a plan for the future. 'Whites in the civil service, too, will soon be migrating to the private sector. They surely realise that, despite the guarantees and the promises of the transition, they are quietly being sidelined, as their predecessors quietly sidelined the English civil servants after 1948. They have much better prospects – and will be much more useful citizens – if they move from wealth consumption to wealth production ... The great mistake of the transition was to attempt to maintain the civil service as a bastion of privilege. It has been preserved, that is true, but the privilege now belongs to the leaders of the ANC, to their lieutenants and satraps, to their allies and favourites. To the ANC the government has become precisely what it was to the Nationalists: a fountain of money, a trough.' Owen could see South Africa's political and economic cycles repeating themselves.

Back in the 1960s, during the heyday of apartheid, the exploitation of cheap labour and plentiful natural resources provided the base for an extraordinary decade when growth averaged 6.9% a year. The National Party government knew it needed to be more self-sufficient after leaving the Commonwealth in 1961, and set about creating industries that would reduce its reliance on global trade. It educated, employed and advanced the interests of Afrikaners as it developed its own manufacturing sector to withstand economic sanctions, which became inevitable particularly after the declaration by the United Nations in 1973 that apartheid was a crime against humanity. Eskom, Armscor and Sasol, among others, were all part of the creation of highly effective, well-run state-owned enterprises as the Afrikaner government built a 20th-century version of the laager, the defensive structures of their ancestors, the Voortrekkers, as they moved into the interior to escape British rule in the 1830s.

Afrikaner businesses were also established with the intention to support the economic aspirations of the *volk*. In 1918, first Santam and then Sanlam were established, followed by the likes of Volkskas and Trust Bank. No one else was going to look after Afrikaner interests but Afrikaners themselves. Memories of the South African War, the defeat of the Boer republics and the horrors of the concentration camps were still fresh in the minds of the early Afrikaner capitalists.

While all white South Africans were beneficiaries of apartheid, whether they supported it at the ballot box or not, it provided particular protections for Afrikaners. It was a system designed by Afrikaners primarily for Afrikaners. Ironically, it was also the very system which not only restricted the potential of black South Africans, but prevented many Afrikaners from reaching their full potential too. They may have had jobs and status, but they could not pit their wits against the world. They may have had political power and held positions of great authority in politics and the civil service, but in reality the economy was so constrained owing to the plethora of rules that few Afrikaners risked starting businesses. There were notable exceptions, of course, the most famous being Anton Rupert. And even those who did break the mould found they had limited markets to serve. With the majority of the population excluded from free enterprise, the white middle-class market was destined to remain small and concentrated and would never provide the growth needed for Afrikaner entrepreneurs to develop multi-billion-rand enterprises.

For businesses seeking markets, it must have been infuriating. Every small town in South Africa, for example, had one bottlestore or more. Typically these would serve different market segments: white residents and 'the rest'. You might have entered the whites-only section to be met with generous self-service displays of Bell's Whisky, Gordon's Gin, Castle Lager and Nederburg wines, while a few metres away, around a dividing wall, would have been a long line of black customers queuing at a counter from which the storekeeper handed out half-jacks of Martell and Richelieu and quarts of Black Label beer. When the bell on the door of the whites-only section would ring, he would invariably stop serving the black customers to attend to the needs of the white client. Not only was it dehumanising to those in the queue, but the rules and regulations of the time also significantly undermined the storekeeper's ability to grow his customer base.

When apartheid ended, many of those protections that cushioned whites fell away, and the result was extraordinary. Freed from the shackles of a system that served only the interests of a minority of the population, Afrikaners were well positioned to exploit the economic benefits of the political liberation of the majority of the country's citizens.

In the early 1990s Frans Meyer and a group of fellow engineering graduates from Stellenbosch were contemplating the future. For these specialised electromagnetic engineers, a natural career path would once have included signing up at one of the Armscor subsidiaries to work on creating sophisticated weapons systems. But the transition to democracy and the impending amalgamation of the South African Defence Force and the military wings of the liberation movements, as well as a slashing of military budgets, meant that this avenue was now closed to them. So they set about creating their own business.

Today, their company Alphawave employs more than 200 people and 120 specialised engineers and scientists in Stellenbosch, and they are world leaders in radio-wave technologies. In addition to creating technologies that help sales managers run cloud-based systems to remotely monitor their reps on the road to see what progress they are making on a daily basis, they also offer radar technology on golf driving ranges to map every single shot played in order to assist coaches to better train their clients.

Oh, and did I mention that they are also mapping space? Signing up clients like Boeing, NASA, Daimler AG and Bosch to provide them with algorithms used in one of their early simulation-software products, they have grown a high-value intellectual-property business in South Africa over 25 years and, as experts on radio waves, are also key service providers to the African mobile telecoms industry. Probably their most impressive achievement to date has been their involvement with the MeerKAT space telescope, which forms part of the Karoo-based Square Kilometre Array (SKA) telescope.

They have also developed the most sensitive radio astronomy receiver in the world, thanks to the powerful use of their simulation-software algorithms and the fundamental design insights of a group of guys who were once considering a career in public service. The SKA will be able to see some 9 billion light years into deep space and, because it will be fifty times more sensitive and can survey the sky ten thousand times faster than any other radio telescope in the world right now, will remain at the forefront of space exploration for a generation.

Using Stellenbosch-designed radio astronomy receivers, astronomers have been better able to understand the universe through identifying new features in our home galaxy that are believed to be millions of years old. The giant bubbles of gas and space debris extend hundreds of light years above and below the centre of the Milky Way. Using the MeerKAT space telescope, astronomers have been able to see unprecedented bright flashes in the galaxy's black hole for the first time.

The head of astrophysics at the University of Oxford, Steven Balbus, told *Nature* magazine: 'This is the nearest supermassive black hole to us in the Universe, and MeerKAT has provided us with front row centre seats. We are going to learn an enormous amount about how black holes feed themselves and how they influence their environments.'

So the algorithms used in the engineering simulation software, and the design itself of the most sensitive radio astronomy receivers in the world, were both created by a group of Stellenbosch-based super-nerds who might otherwise have ended up creating highly effective military systems. Instead they are helping astronomers piece together a galactic fossil record, and will assist us in understanding our place in the universe.

Not only that but in January 2020 Skynamo, a subsidiary of Alphawave, secured a $30m capital injection from US software investor Five Elms Capital to expand its technology, which helps companies manage remote sales forces, into the US market. With

operations in South Africa and the UK, it is opening a new head-
quarters in Atlanta. Using the Stellenbosch brains trust, it has
developed software that allows mobile sales forces to automate
administrative tasks and digitise paper processes, speeding up the
feedback loop to executives and thus enabling them to make better, speedier strategic decisions.

South Africa's most successful global company, Naspers, had
its origins in the Afrikaner capitalism that first emerged a hundred
years ago. Its roots lie in the creation of Sanlam and Santam, both
still major players in both long-term and short-term insurance,
and of Volkskas, which would later become a cornerstone of
Absa bank. Naspers could have remained a successful media business serving its core market. Critical to the success and growth
of Afrikaner capitalism was control of the media – at that time,
the big Afrikaans newspaper titles, in which members of the *volk*
were encouraged to support businesses and enterprises run by
Afrikaners. But Naspers had bigger ambitions.

During the apartheid era Naspers was massively influential,
but not particularly valuable. By the time Nelson Mandela was
released from prison on 11 February 1990, Naspers was not one
of the Top 40 companies on the JSE. However, a single transaction 11 years later would eventually lead to its becoming South
Africa's most valuable business and would spawn the biggest technology company listed on the Euronext exchange in Amsterdam.

Naspers saw the opportunity presented by the Chinese economy's miraculous growth in the 1990s and made several poor
investments, insisting initially on putting its own people in charge
of projects and then quickly learning this was not the way to get

ahead in China. It was poised to return home bloodied and beaten when a final roll of the die and a single $32m bet on a stake in a company whose business was direct messaging on mobile devices turned into a boon not only for directors of the company, but also for all investors on the JSE. The $32m grew in value to over $133bn. At its peak that single stock made up nearly 20% of the value of all the shares listed on the JSE.

Koos Bekker joined the newspaper group in 1985, fresh from obtaining an MBA at Columbia University in New York, where he had done his thesis on the pay-TV market, particularly the cable company HBO, which was a trailblazer in getting its customers to pay for content. Television had only arrived in South Africa in 1976, and, as with so much else, the country was decades behind the rest of the world. Bekker launched M-Net and later DStv, which became a pan-African broadcaster. The latter was spun off in late 2018 into the separately listed MultiChoice, which today boasts some 18 million customers, 10 million of whom are outside South Africa. Pay TV would provide the capital Naspers needed to make internet investments, and Bekker freely admits that choosing Tencent in 2001 was the luckiest deal of his life. The Naspers acquisition of what is now a 30% stake in Tencent meant that the firm's directors hit pay-dirt.

Famously, Bekker sacrificed a monthly pay cheque for share options and was CEO of Naspers for 17 years from 1997 to 2014. It was during a sabbatical, after retiring as CEO, that he sold most of his Naspers shares. Because he wasn't an office-bearer in the company at the time, he avoided the need to publicly disclose the sale or the price he achieved for his stock. It made him eye-wateringly rich and he joined the illustrious Forbes list of dollar billionaires. He would later return as chairman and oversee the unbundling of Naspers's global businesses.

Forbes magazine billed Bekker as the Rupert Murdoch of Africa. It's not clear if this was meant as a compliment. Murdoch at the peak of his power was a high-stakes political player and had significant influence by means of his media platforms over the politics of the UK. Bekker, in contrast, was more intent on building a developing-markets internet empire and succeeded in doing so in a relatively short time. He openly admits to being lucky in backing Tencent. After all, he'd kissed a lot of frogs before one turned into a handsome prince. While Naspers runs a large and impressive media business with a mix of newspapers and digital technologies delivering content across Africa from its base in South Africa, this is just a small part of the business and gets little of the attention that the high-margin, money-making e-commerce services attract.

During 2019 Naspers decided to unbundle the group's global internet businesses into a new Amsterdam listing called Prosus, Latin for 'forwards'. Following the unbundling, Naspers still owns about 70% of the issued shares in the new company. Naspers's own shareholding is far more opaque, but its Tencent investment has provided it with a strong base from which to acquire stakes in internet businesses around the world.

Another of South Africa's biggest investment successes was PSG. Started by stockbroker Jannie Mouton, who was famously fired by his friends and colleagues at Senekal, Mouton and Kitshoff for being hard to work with, it has been one of the most extraordinary investments in the world for much of the past 25 years.

In his book *En toe fire hulle my* (*And then they fired me*) Mouton tells how after being fired he stayed at home for two years trying to figure out what to do next. He knew stockbroking, understood financial markets and had an uncanny knack for spotting opportunities.

Rather than roll up in a ball and capitulate, he started reading voraciously and making notes of the lessons he learned, most notably from Warren Buffett, whose investment philosophy was similar to his own. He took time to do a not-always-honest introspection, through his own SWOT analysis, and when he told his wife that he found he had far more positives than negatives, she sent him back to fill in the forms again.

Mouton finally decided he would build a financial-sector firm listed on the JSE that would generate the capital he needed to fund his ambition. He paid R3.5m for 51% of the listed recruitment business PAG – Professional Assignments Group. That formed the foundation of the empire. He was able to sell that stake for R52.5m three years later. By then PSG was gaining attention. Investors were buying the story and rivals were circling. The scariest moment came when Absa, concerned that PSG was mopping up its core Afrikaner market, made a hostile takeover bid. It was at that point that Markus Jooste, now infamous for his role in the collapse of Steinhoff, stepped in and bought a 17% share of the company. It made the firm secure from a hostile takeover. Directors of the company owned a third of its stock; friends and family owned a slice; and with Jooste on board, Mouton felt he had the security he needed with 62.5% of issued shares in what he regarded as safe hands. Mouton proved to be an extraordinary deal-maker, creating the building blocks of a business worth R55bn on the JSE today.

If you'd invested R10,000 each into Amazon and PSG in August 1996, which investment would have earned you more today? To make the question a bit more interesting, let's add the S&P 500, JSE Top 40 Index and Warren Buffett's Berkshire Hathaway into the mix. If you don't remember 1996, ask an older relative and he or she will explain some of its oddities.

Imagine you were given R10,000 and told you could have it on one condition: you had to invest it all in one of five options. Remember, we're talking 1996 here. Take yourself back to that time, and don't be like audiences on whom I have tested this who immediately think of the world today and make their choice. Go back to 1996.

First option: a company run by a guy who is becoming increasingly famous. He's converted an old textile-milling company into an investment firm. He could afford to live far better than he does, but has chosen to stay, by billionaire standards, in a relatively modest home in the nicest part of the sprawling city of Omaha in Nebraska. His company is Berkshire Hathaway.

Second option: S&P 500. This gives great diversification across 500 of the most valuable companies in the US. The S&P 500 has the reputation of being the greatest measure of American economic success. It incorporates all 30 companies of the Dow Jones Industrial Average, the most quoted stock market index in the world, but the fact that it is an index of the 500 most valuable publicly listed American companies means you get great exposure to the mighty US economy.

Third option: the JSE. Indexation is yet to become a thing on the JSE. But as this is just a game, play along. Putting your R10,000 into South Africa is a big bet on the future. Nelson Mandela is president of the country. The Government of National Unity has fallen apart and former president FW de Klerk has taken the National Party out of the arrangement agreed to in the negotiations leading up to the country's first democratic elections. Trevor Manuel, a former construction worker, is finance minister, and the former labour minister Tito Mboweni, responsible for overseeing some of the world's most onerous labour policies, is the Reserve Bank governor. The country is still not rated as investment grade while the new ANC government shifts economic policy towards greater free-market principles.

Fourth option: Amazon. Bear in mind it's 1996, and connecting to the internet in South Africa requires you to plug your computer into a modem, and the modem into your telephone line, at which point you dial a number to give you access to this new thing called 'the internet'.

There is some crazy guy in the US called Jeff Bezos who thinks the internet is going to revolutionise not only the way we shop in the future, but also the way we live, interact and buy stuff. The guy's clearly off his rocker. I mean, who is going to wait ages for a page to download (what does that even mean?) and then click on a book cover you have not even flicked through or opened, and buy it through a website? And he expects you to give information about yourself, even your credit card details. Surely this can never work. Why would anyone do this when you can walk into one of the many perfectly good bookshops and browse through thousands of titles and take home with you a choice of books, immediately? Next thing they're going to tell you that video shops are about to be overtaken and that you will be able to stream content to your phone. Whatever next? But, hey, it's your R10,000.

Option 5: PSG. This is the outlier. Its founder is a guy who made his name in stockbroking and until two years ago was a partner in a stock brokerage in Johannesburg. You've heard through the grapevine that he is razor sharp, his English language skills are not his strongpoint, and he has the reputation for being difficult to work with – so much so that he arrived at work one morning to find himself summoned to the boardroom where a group of men he considered his friends fired him. He sat at home for about two years licking his wounds until one day he made his first acquisition, a recruitment firm called PAG.

After all five options are considered, it turns out your money was best invested in a little-known South African start-up called PSG.

The options delivered the following growth rates:

- S&P 500: 9% – making the R10,000 worth about R280,000 today.
- Berkshire Hathaway: 10% – giving you R370,000 today.
- JSE Top 40: 12% – giving you R536,000 today, or nearly twice what you earned on the US market.
- Amazon: 31% – giving you an extraordinary R20m.
- PSG: it grew at a compound annual growth rate of 36% – giving you a staggering R55m.

PSG is still heavily reliant on the performance of its biggest investment, Capitec. Capitec saw a gap in the market that was not being served by the established banks and launched itself as a microlender, primarily making short-term loans at high interest rates to mostly black customers. People came in their droves, seeking to escape the clutches of the informal sector where collection methods can be forceful, and entered the formal borrowing market for the first time.

The apartheid state would never have condoned the existence of a Capitec in its current form. It needed to wait for democracy to exist. Much the same is true of Curro, the private-schools business, which serves a broad demographic of South Africans wary of the failings of public education. Founder Chris van der Merwe himself built the first school at his local church and then another. Later he realised that he was going to need serious capital to fund the expansion of the business. He went to a PSG exco meeting.

'Halfway through the meeting,' Van der Merwe says, 'Jannie Mouton pushed his chair back from the table. I thought I had lost him. Instead he committed to invest personally in Curro and said it was up to the team to decide if PSG would back us.' They did, and the rest is history. Van der Merwe is now focusing his attention on building Stadio, a business that will provide tertiary education in a market that needs investment. In 1994 universities educated about 300,000 young (mostly white) students. That number has expanded to over a million today and demand for places outstrips supply. PSG has been good at spotting market trends and catching the wave. Across many of its businesses, its clientele is mostly made up of black South Africans. Its empowerment model would not have been tolerated by the National Party government.

Unlike Old Mutual, which barrelled into developed markets soon after listing on the JSE and bought up anything that wasn't nailed down at full price, Sanlam was far more circumspect in its international expansion, entering into partnerships in Malaysia and India before embarking on a shape-shifting deal with Saham Insurance in Morocco, which gave it a footprint of operations in 33 countries across the continent. It's a far cry from the early days soon after its unbundling and listing on the JSE when the firm appeared at death's door. It was a (s)lumbering giant. It moved slowly, while the world moved quickly.

Perhaps that lack of agility is what saved it from an Old Mutual-style spending spree. At that time 85% of its business came from white Afrikaners and it had very little presence outside the Western Cape. And as pension funds switched to defined-contribution funds from old-style defined benefits, Sanlam floundered. It sold a stake in Absa to raise capital, brought in Patrice Motsepe and the Batho Bonke Trust as empowerment partners, and suddenly Sanlam was back in the game, moving from an apartheid dinosaur to a 21st-century South African company.

Sanlam, once the bastion of Afrikaner capitalism, had come of age and reinvented itself as a more nimble player in developing markets with a strong presence across the African continent. Time will tell whether its strategy is one that wins. But it is certain that had it not changed its outlook, it would probably no longer exist.

CHAPTER 4

The amazing South African stock market

'Rule number 1: Never lose money.
Rule number 2: Don't forget rule number 1.' – Warren Buffett

In 2002 there were about 480 companies listed on the JSE. Today there are about 360, and the listing's pipeline has slowed to a trickle. Stock markets exist so that companies can raise capital and, despite the downsizing, the JSE remains one of the world's better-regulated, better-run and most respected markets. It is not alone in this trend. Corporate failures, listings and delistings are perfectly normal. World Bank figures show that in the US the number of publicly listed companies is down by 50% over 20 years and there are similar trends in Europe. It's not that there have been massive 1930s Great Depression-style failures. What has happened is that in many cases private-equity players have moved in and bought undervalued companies and worked them hard to deliver superlative returns, out of the public spotlight. There have also been changes in the way that companies raise capital. There is a lot more private money going into businesses than previously.

The performance of companies listed on the JSE has been poor over the past five years or so, with returns barely beating inflation, while US markets in their longest bull run in history are trading at record levels. There the pain taken in the 2008 market crash has all but been forgotten. At home, foreigners have sold South African assets in record numbers – more than R300bn worth in 2019 alone – the most in a decade. Foreigners have been net sellers of South African bonds and equities since 2016 after being quite finely balanced. There was a small flurry of bond buying during the Ramaphoria period, but that quickly reversed as it became apparent just how toxic the investing environment had become.

Up to 1994, the ownership of South Africa's economy was massively concentrated in just a few hands. Large companies in those days almost fulfilled the role that private-equity firms do today. Anglo American owned everything from wine farms to media houses, banks and insurers, and lots of mines, in South Africa. SAB was also a big industrial shareholder in the closed economy and ended up owning lots of non-brewing businesses, including OK Bazaars, which it famously sold to Whitey Basson for R1, enabling Shoprite to cement its hold on lower-income customers.

While there has been a sea change in the listed environment, it's still vital for ordinary investors, whether they buy shares in their personal capacity or purchase unit trusts or simply participate in the company pension scheme. Markets matter. Their performance is also important for anyone who hopes to have a chance of retiring one day.

Quick pub quiz question for you. (Don't peek down the page.

That's cheating.) Which country had the world's best-performing stock market for 117 years from 1900 to 2017?

There are three options for you:

(1) South Africa
(2) United States
(3) Australia

And the correct answer is: (1) South Africa!

Don't believe me?

The current political and economic environment has dampened expectations in South Africa, according to macroeconomic data, such as the business confidence index, which, after festering at its lowest levels in a generation, finally ticked up a notch in November 2019. The current environment, by any measure, is not great.

However, when you look at the performance of the local equity market over the past century, it could be that our expectations are too low. From 1900 to the end of 2017, the South African market was the best-performing in the world, delivering an average annual return of inflation plus 7.2%. This is according to the 2017 edition of the *Credit Suisse Global Investment Returns Yearbook*, which compared the returns of various asset classes over 117 years in 21 countries with a continuous investment history. This might seem hard to believe. Given the country's political history and economic difficulties, how could South Africa have been the best-performing stock market in the world since the turn of the 20th century?

Free markets dictate that companies with high returns on

capital attract competition. Rising competition causes the balance of supply and demand to shift, driving down the prices of goods and services. As industry margins begin to narrow, returns on capital start to fall. In contrast, a lack of competition allows companies to continue earning excess returns on capital for extended periods. That was one of the factors in South African investors' favour. Along with serious inflation through the 1980s, the commodity boom of the 1970s when South Africa was the world's biggest gold supplier to global markets, and the fact that local companies faced less competition compared with their peers in many other countries, it added to performance. This last factor was the result of prolonged periods of political uncertainty, of sanctions during much of the apartheid era, and of a persistent fear that South Africa would suffer a similar fate to Zimbabwe.

Then came 1994. South African companies had been gradually welcomed back into the international fold after the unbanning of political organisations and the release of Nelson Mandela in 1990. The period between 1990 and 1994 was arguably one of the most uncertain in modern South African history. Talks between the National Party government and former liberation movements were never guaranteed to deliver a peaceful settlement, and while the world knew the ANC would win the 1994 elections, no one had any idea of what shape the economy would take. With almost indecent haste, South African companies began diversifying offshore as soon as they could.

Prior to 1990 the South African economy was inwardly focused. On the JSE, 33 out of 40 businesses were mining companies, 23 of them gold miners. Of the top 40 companies listed on the JSE in 1990, only a handful survive today, and only three, Anglo American, Richemont and Remgro, are still in the Top 40, which today is far more services-based. Three-quarters of the companies on the Top 40 today either did not exist on the day Mandela walked free from Victor Verster Prison, or were in the earliest stages of their development. The latter include today's giants, Bidvest, Massmart, Shoprite, Pick n Pay and the Foschini Group. Companies like cellphone giants Vodacom and MTN did not exist, and when they were launched in 1993 and 1994, it was assumed there was only a market for some 80,000 handsets in South Africa. That number proved to be a gross miscalculation. On the day Mandela was released from prison, Capitec did not exist, Jannie Mouton was happily ensconced in a stockbroking company with some of his closest friends, the banks were too small to be in the Top 40, and Naspers was a Cape Town-based publisher of books, magazines and newspapers. The idea that in less than a decade the country would have satellite TV seemed a pipe dream.

How things have changed.

Today, about 70% of the profits of JSE-listed companies are generated offshore. While many companies have made poor acquisitions over time, there has been a gradual shift in company earnings to sources outside South Africa. Naspers, and its recently unbundled Prosus, gained scale through the acquisition of Tencent. They alone make up between 17% and 20% of the value of all the shares on the JSE, thanks to the dramatic growth the Chinese company has seen from its early days as an instant-messaging platform to its current status as one of the world's premier online-game developers.

The top 40 companies on the JSE now account for 90% of the total value of the shares listed on the market. The six biggest alone make up 60% of the value. All the same, it's important to realise that some of the companies are global players and not South African, but have listings on the JSE for historical reasons. The Ruperts' role in the creation of Richemont and British American Tobacco, for example, means that South African investors have been given access to the profits of some of the world's biggest luxury goods makers and cigarette firms, while Naspers's performance is by no means a reflection of anything to do with the South African economy.

The economy is far more diversified than it was on the day Nelson Mandela was released from prison. Back then, 33 of the top 40 companies on the JSE were resources firms. As South Africa opened up to the world and companies globalised, there was also a consolidation of old industries, and the small mining companies of the past were consolidated primarily into what are Harmony and Sibanye today.

There is no doubt that the top 40 of the JSE today offer a far greater smorgasbord of investment options than back in the 1980s. They comprise a mixture of banks, insurers, retailers, cellphone companies, private hospital groups, pharmaceuticals companies and property firms.

So much of market performance depends on when you start measuring. Pick a starting time five years ago, and it will be hard to beat the performance of the US market. Pick a point 21 years ago, and Russia is the star performer. The starting point matters when it comes to defining returns over fixed periods of time. Russia experienced a financial crisis in 1998 along with all other so-called emerging markets; this led to a collapse in the value of the rouble, a substantial outflow of foreign investment and, as in South Africa in 1987, a freeze on debt repayments.

Nevertheless, Russia made tough, smart choices in getting its economy back on track, and over the past 21 years has outperformed all other stock markets in dollar terms. While the S&P 500 grew at a creditable 336% between September 1998 and June 2019, the Nasdaq, despite the dot-com bubble burst in the early 2000s, was up 484% and the MSCI Emerging Markets Index was up 584% over the same period. The MSCI Russia Index, on the other hand, grew (from a low base, of course) 3,366% over that time – an average annual compounded return of 18.4% a year.

Timing is everything. Had you bought into Russia a year before the market bottomed, you would have done considerably worse, as you would have invested at higher levels. Picking bottoms is impossible, and few, if any, people would have committed $1,000 to the Russian market on 20 September 1998 and left it there. The country was in trouble; money was leaving in floods; investors had lost hope in the future. The situation seemed unfixable. Russia, still so new after the fall of the Berlin Wall, was as vulnerable as any financially distressed country could be, but investors who had faith and kept it were handsomely rewarded for their trouble.

It is safe to say that few South Africans would believe that the country has ever been a decent place to invest.

What would R1,000 invested in the JSE on the day Hendrik Verwoerd took South Africa out of the Commonwealth in 1961 be worth today?

Arguably, a person approaching 60 today could have had parents with considerable foresight who invested the money for their child on what must have felt like a serious low point in the economy and the society. The only instruction they might have given is that the money should not be touched and all dividends needed to be reinvested. What would that money be worth today?

By the end of the 1960s, a decade when growth averaged over 6% a year, the money would have grown four times and be worth R4,200.

The next decade, characterised by considerably lower growth, at least one recession, a spiralling oil price, rising social discontent manifested in the 1976 Soweto student uprising, and the tightening of the country's draconian security apparatus, should have seen lower returns. But the money grew in value nearly five times to just under R20,000.

The 1980s must go down in history as one of the most divisive and difficult in South Africa. After PW Botha's Rubicon speech in 1985, when he defied the world and seemed to reject reform, the economy went into a downward spiral. Overseas banks refused to extend credit and the country defaulted on its debt. Companies with foreign debts collapsed. Former Nedbank CEO Tom Boardman, who'd created a homeware store styled on international trends, was forced to sell the chain named after him, and Christo Wiese was forced to financially re-engineer Pep to avoid disaster. It was a rough decade of oppression and violence. Yet by the end of it, the money invested in 1961 would have grown to around R190,000.

FirstRand co-founder GT Ferreira describes the aftermath of the Rubicon speech as one of the best periods for the fledgling business he'd started with Laurie Dippenaar and Paul Harris. It created the environment which saw Barclays divest from the country. In this way an opportunity was opened for the three 'wise men', as they are referred to today, to buy not only the insurer Southern Life from Anglo American, but First National Bank (Barclays's successor) as well. There was a far darker time in 2008 when Ferreira received a call from Dippenaar one evening, asking whether they would be able to open for business the next day as inter-bank trust had collapsed and banks were too scared to deposit money with each other for fear that their partner bank might be the next to collapse. Compared to that, the mid-1980s were, according to Ferreira, a doddle.

Chaos, the ancient Chinese strategist Sun Tzu wrote, most certainly does create opportunity.

So, after 30 years invested in the stock market that R1,000 had grown in value to R190,000. What is it worth today? (At this stage it's probably fair to point out that R1,000 in 1961 terms is worth about R75,000 today, so this is purely an academic exercise, as very few families would have had that kind of money available for an investment for their child.) So the first three decades were good. You made a return 190 times the value of the original investment. Considering how awful returns have been over the past five years, how much money might be in the pot?

'South Africa's state performance peaked in 2007, that year its economy and governance were at their best. Since then the state has experienced continuous decline in all core indicators of performance,' the risk agency Eunomix said in a statement in 2019. 'The developmental state project has failed. South Africa is now a fragile state, expected to continue to weaken.'

Despite that, the JSE has continued to perform. That's because the JSE is more globally diversified today than ever before. Remember Naspers and its 'lucky' Tencent deal? Naspers went from being a small-town publisher to listing the biggest technology company on the Euronext exchange in 2019, in less than 20 years. The expansion of South African companies internationally means that with varying degrees of success, the biggest South African companies listed on the JSE earn more outside the country than they did over three decades locally. Tencent was just the luck the company needed. It was also a very welcome boost to the value of JSE portfolios as at one point it made up about 20% of the total value of shares on the JSE.

The bottom line, as far as JSE returns are concerned, is that managers have always been able to find a way around the macroeconomic environment. The lack of competition has kept margins high. The tough economic and policy climate has further discouraged competition. In times of distress, and there have been plenty, South African companies have tended to flourish at the expense of the newcomers. Tough environments make the survivors stronger. Weak players either get absorbed or leave the market completely as the winners grab their share of the available spoils.

So what is that original R1,000 investment worth today?

(a) R760,000
(b) R7.6m
(c) R17.6m
Answer: (b) R7.6m

That is a compound annual growth rate of 19.34%. Given that the economy grew in a context of limited competition, and that the global gates opened to South Africa as communism was coming to an end in Eastern Europe, investors have seen a double benefit over time.

A Bank of America survey of South Africa's 12 biggest fund managers in the final quarter of 2019 found that the highest number since 2011 regarded the country's shares as cheap, while a similar number regarded the country's bonds as offering value. It's the first positive indicator in years that investment outflows, which spiked in 2019, might be reversed in 2020 as expectations for economic growth improve, even if only marginally.

The bank's head of Emerging Market Cross-Asset Research and Economics, David Hauner, suggested there might be an opportunity for investors in South African markets. As always the suggestion comes with a caveat: 'Foreign investors are lightly positioned and this could be an opportunity if things fall into place.' But investors, both local and foreign, want to see growth. The opportunity of tying up money in South Africa, regardless of the cheap valuations, when it could be generating a real return elsewhere, can only be realised when there is a fair degree of economic certainty. Interestingly, the risk of a credit downgrade in 2020 was already priced into markets, meaning that the opportunity for making decent returns still exists.

There are no guarantees and T&Cs most certainly do apply. Unless South Africa gets another substantial boost, it's hard to see how it could achieve a performance even close to historical levels – unless, just unless the Africa growth story does play out in the way its citizens hope it might.

In late November 2019, Twitter CEO Jack Dorsey announced he would be making Africa his home for at least three months in 2020 because he sees its potential for the future. He'd travelled through South Africa, Ghana, Nigeria and Ethiopia meeting entrepreneurs, and was clearly impressed. His announcement in a tweet, naturally, read: 'Sad to be leaving the continent … for now. Africa will define the future (especially the bitcoin one). Not sure where yet, but I'll be living here for 3–6 months mid-2020. Grateful I was able to experience a small part.'

Africa needs foreign direct investment, and when the normally publicity-shy Patrice Motsepe openly praised Donald Trump at Davos in January 2020, saying 'Africa loves America. Africa loves you,' he was rightly lambasted for assuming to speak for a population of 1.35 billion people, a growing number of whom are under 25 and struggling to survive, never mind thriving economically.

While apologising for claiming to speak on behalf of the continent, he emphasised in a statement: 'My remarks … were partly aimed at encouraging discussions between the Trump Administration and African political and business leaders, particularly in the context of the increasing feedback from certain American political and business leaders that South Africa and some African countries are anti-America and its political leadership. This perception has had an impact on our ability to attract foreign investments and create jobs.'

The Africa opportunity does require a strong and stable launch pad. South Africa has long been that place but it runs the risk of losing that commercial advantage to faster-growing, more stable, safer, and better geographically located regions. The launch pad could remain South Africa, but this country needs to get its fundamentals in shape first – and fast.

CHAPTER 5

South Africa's inequality crisis

'Let them eat cake.' – Marie Antoinette

South Africa is a fundamentally unfair country. You can call it unequal if you want but that doesn't quite cover it. Unfair is a better descriptor. Not 'unfair', as when a child is admonished for something bad that a sibling did; but 'unfair' in the dictionary sense: 'not based on or behaving according to the principles of equality and justice'. Synonyms include words like 'unjust' or 'inequitable'. Why those words are better ways of describing the huge disparities that exist in South Africa is that the moment you change the way you think about a problem, the more you are obliged to do something about it.

Describing a society as 'unequal' implies that it's a fact of life, that there's nothing that can be done about it. Inequality has always existed. It's a fact of life everywhere. All societies have an elite. In most cases that elite is multi-generational and wealth is handed down through the ages. You can resign yourself to the inevitability that some people are just born lucky.

The moment you look at the economics of a country like

South Africa and describe it as 'unfair' or 'unjust', the conversation is changed. You may not be able to fix inequality, but you can surely take steps to ensure a fairer society. In many respects, that's what several ANC administrations have sought to do through numerous policy interventions since 1994. There has been some progress but not nearly enough, primarily because policy interventions have been made at the expense of the rich rather than through a pro-growth economic policy which would have lifted far more people out of the depths of financial despair.

The introduction of social grants was a first step in ensuring the country's poorest citizens were given a chance of survival. The expansion of public health care and schooling was intended to ensure that even the poorest in society would be able to gain access to the basic services any country should supply its citizens. However, the government has done a really bad job at ensuring those services are the best they could be.

If you run a business or are employed in a job that gives you disposable income, you immediately have more choices than the poorest 80% of the country. The mere fact that you have a job puts you in an elite club, and if you have medical aid and a company pension scheme thrown into the mix, you are winning, regardless of how you feel about your personal circumstances at this moment.

Medical aid gives one access to some of the best hospitals in the world, and, depending on how much you earn, your children can attend some of the best schools on the continent. Through a subscription to a private security service you are better protected than those who have to rely on the overstretched police.

The private-security sector employs more than three times as many people as there are in the police force. Privilege thus buys security, education, health and lifestyle whereas most people in the country have to rely on the state. Other than a few pockets of excellence, the state is failing miserably and exacerbating the already significant divides.

To suggest that there has been no change in inequality over the last quarter of a century is not true. A report by Stats SA on economic indicators between 2006 and 2015 concluded that inequality is extremely high and has remained so since 1993. Both conclusions are correct, but they imply there has been no change. The economist Brian Kantor points out that in 2006 the top 10% of earners in South Africa made 12.5 times more than the bottom 40%. By 2015 that ratio had declined to 10.2. No one is suggesting for a moment that the inequality levels in South Africa are acceptable. But we do need to acknowledge that there has been an improvement largely as a result of the country's progressive tax system and the redistribution of some of that wealth by means of the social grants system, which has lifted millions out of abject poverty. Without growth to keep the cash flows running, that mechanism of distribution is, however, rapidly running out of steam.

The only way to truly tackle inequality is to generate economic growth, which creates jobs, brings more people into the working class, and helps established households migrate into the middle-income segment. There is no magic wand. But some politically unpalatable decisions do have to be taken that will allow skilled migrants into the country, control the immigration of unskilled people, and, horror of horrors, encourage the creation of small businesses by easing some of the policy restrictions to make life easier for start-ups to, well, start up.

South Africa's regulatory regime was designed for large corporations, but for small businesses of a certain size, say with turnovers of R10m, R20m or R50m, the requirements can be off-putting. The upside of that complexity for incumbents is that it keeps competition out as it discourages rivals. That too creates an ever-larger chasm between those who have and those who do not. Unless South Africa can think fundamentally differently about its inequality crisis, it is condemning future generations to more of the same with potentially disastrous consequences.

South Africa's economy is dominated by large corporates and conglomerates. Beyond a few notable exceptions, they don't grow by creating jobs; they grow through productivity gains. Because these large companies have established a dominant position in a concentrated range of industries, they make it hard for anyone else to break in, and as a result we have a situation where there is jobless growth.

South Africa has one of the lowest levels of social mobility on earth. If you are born poor and live in one of the country's many sprawling townships, you are more than likely to die there in similar economic circumstances. In the same way, if you are born into privilege and play by the rules, you are likely to remain better off. The skewed ownership of assets as well as the skewed engagement of people in jobs means that your odds of changing your fate are small. Tragically, inspiring stories of young people who grew up in poor households and managed to rise to the upper echelons of business are rare. They exist, but they are not common.

What can be done? Over the past decade the government has attempted to roll out the developmental state but it has failed lamentably. FirstRand chairman Roger Jardine, once the youngest director-general when he ran the Department of Arts, Culture, Science and Technology in the Mandela years, wrote in his 2019 chairman's statement: 'Perhaps the time has come to acknowledge that a South African developmental state for the twenty-first century must strongly position the private sector as a key partner to the state in the industrial transformation of our country.'

Jardine might have been (metaphorically) burned at the stake for such heresy five years ago, but there is now growing acceptance that government cannot go it alone and needs help. The brutal reality is that you do not create economic opportunity in a vacuum. Jobs are the result of a productive environment in which smart people are incentivised to risk capital in order to grow enterprises that do create jobs. If the overall environment is not conducive to growth, jobs are impossible to create.

'We need to stop obsessing or even fussing about ownership of companies,' says the economist Dr Adrian Saville, CEO of Cannon Asset Managers. 'It doesn't matter who owns a company. The only question is, does this company have the capacity to sustain itself to do something productive? What I mean by that is that it can be foreign owned, domestic owned, it can be publicly owned, it can be privately owned, it can be listed or unlisted. It could be part of a conglomerate, it could be a stand-alone, it could be family owned: ownership really doesn't matter. The question that we have to put first is: is this a viable entity? And if it's a viable entity, you now have the prospect of establishing employment inside that viable entity.'

International research shows time and time again that it is the smaller companies that create jobs. According to studies undertaken by Cannon Asset Managers over a 20-year period, the largest companies on the JSE created very few jobs while the smaller firms had a considerable multiplier effect on employment. The problem is that there are just too few of them.

Government regularly pays lip service to the notion of people starting their own businesses. Considering the bureaucratic red tape involved in getting a company registered, and a host of compliance and regulatory issues that demand attention, it's a wonder small businesses ever start, never mind grow.

The economist Xhanti Payi, who runs his own consultancy, Nascence Advisory, once told me: 'Telling young people that the solution to their unemployment is to build their own business is nothing more than a cruel hoax.' It's a damning criticism of an economic system that lets young people down at every turn. Even considering that in healthy start-up markets the vast majority of businesses will fail within five years, Payi's criticisms appear well founded.

South Africa finds itself in a classic chicken-and-egg situation. The country requires entrepreneurial endeavour. For that, risk-takers want at least a modicum of certainty in respect of the policy environment. Starting a business is hard enough, particularly when it comes to raising capital to ensure that you are able to exploit the opportunity you see in the market. The truth is that government needs to get the capital in private hands working. It can do this in two ways. It can tax that money and do the work itself or it can incentivise people who made the money in the first place to use that capital to create new enterprises and in the process produce jobs and thus allow more people to become socially mobile. But the government seems to have an allergy to the rich, believing that their wealth was generated at the expense of others without a fair distribution of the returns for labour. You can go around in circles on this and get nowhere. As for taxing the wealthy to reduce the gap between rich and poor, it's been tried and has largely failed.

Some people, like French economist Thomas Piketty, argue that the rich should be taxed out of existence and propose a global wealth tax. Other economists, like Emmanuel Saez and Gabriel Zucman, have helped Democratic US presidential hopeful Elizabeth Warren design proposals that will see top incomes taxed at a rate of 80%. Could it work? Tax the Oppenheimers, Ruperts, Motsepes and others to the extent that they go from very rich to rich? Unfortunately there are not enough disgustingly rich individuals in South Africa to provide sufficient money to make the exercise worthwhile. It wouldn't change their lifestyles. It wouldn't force them out of their homes. They would still live opulent lives. Just how useful would it be?

The three economists cited above all hail from France, a country that has imposed super-taxes on its richest citizens, but it's barely had an impact. Politically, it was a smart move. It raised the overall tax revenue by a paltry 1% and at the same time 10,000 citizens, including the actor Gérard Depardieu, and the chairman of luxury goods group LVMH, Bernard Arnault, relocated to friendlier jurisdictions, taking their money with them. The socialist government of François Hollande imposed a super-tax on incomes over €1m in 2012. It was repealed two years later amid fears that it would crush France's entrepreneurial spirit. Footballers had also threatened to go on strike over the measures. Inequality may have been reduced on paper, but was France better off as a result?

The short answer: '*Non!*'

You might argue that South Africa needs rebuilding and that the short-term injection of money derived from a wealth and super-tax would give the country a Red Bull-type boost to get the rusty cogs of growth moving again. But the South African state has proved worse than useless at capital allocation, and has persisted in funding failing public enterprises even when private sector funders started to balk at throwing good money after bad. The most recent example of this is the decision by the Development Bank of Southern Africa (DBSA) to provide bankrupt SAA with an injection of R3.5bn. It takes a very broad interpretation of the DBSA mandate to treat SAA as a developmental asset. For the influential trade union grouping Cosatu, the problem is simple: use public-sector workers' pensions as a veritable piggy bank to prop up state failures. All this will do in the world of defined-benefit pension funds is postpone the liability for the state to some future date when pensioners, whose money would have been frittered away by then on funding frivolous failures, will demand their payouts.

The unions are in fact barking at the wrong gate. The conversation they appear incapable of having is the one that requires them to allow the substantial restructuring and commercially minded management of state businesses. Over time this would facilitate a recovery that would create more jobs than exist presently, but they are unwilling to absorb the inevitable short-term pain that proper decision-making would involve.

The problem with distributing the money from taxes rather than keeping it in the hands of growth-hungry entrepreneurs is that it won't be spent where it can deliver the best return. Allow an entrepreneur to risk his or her capital on a venture that will create jobs, become profitable and pay a reasonable rate of tax, and the rewards for the country over the longer term are not just higher, but also more sustainable. What is more, though there is no question that taxes properly applied can make a huge difference in the lives of beneficiaries, the South African government has lost the trust of the tax-paying public to do so effectively, efficiently and without wholesale looting. The second Zuma administration destroyed so much public trust.

Most South African start-ups are created by 40-something year olds, says Pavlo Phitidis at Aurik Business Accelerator. These are people who either through design or default find themselves outside the corporate world and use the skills gleaned in large companies to venture out on their own. Often it's because they have seen an opportunity in the sector they serve and know just how best to exploit it. By the time they get to create their start-up, they would have developed a reputation and connections that give them a better chance of convincing a backer to support their idea. In South Africa, few 20 year olds have those networks or the experience to go out on their own, even if they wanted to. And with youth unemployment raging at over 50%, few of them are ever going to find the job that provides the experience that puts them in the position one day to create their own business. This explains why so many small businesses cannot grow beyond survivalist stage.

Even among corporate employees, the odds in a stagnant economy of their voluntarily leaving a secure job for a start-up is unlikely considering that once they have made the leap out of a large company, they are unlikely to land a job at the same level again as companies are reluctant to hire someone who has shown a propensity to jump ship and has big demands in terms of pay.

There is plenty of international research that demonstrates just how important getting a first job is in determining a person's likely career success. The first job teaches skills and the kind of work ethic that schools usually fail to impart. Showing up on time, completing a series of tasks, burning the midnight oil (and being remunerated appropriately) are qualities tragically in short supply.

That first job is the most important determinant of long-term independence. Without economic participation, there can be no upward mobility, and without that, there is very little chance that South Africa will be able to solve the multiple problems it faces.

For any start-up, access to capital is a significant constraint. In many societies with high savings rates, young people with a bright idea may be able to tap into the bank of Mum and Dad – less politely, fools, friends and family. If you come from a poor community you are considerably less likely to have access to the sort of people who may be able to help you. The inequality crisis is perpetuated through access.

What this means is that the entire architecture of the economy has to be changed. South Africa's economy excludes too many people from participating actively, which explains why government is so fixated with the idea of inclusive growth and of staying in charge of the problem despite its obvious inability to solve it.

'We remain a low-trust society, with a big deficit between what each of us believes and thinks the goals for South Africa should be. If we are going to get a prosperous outcome in which we are all engaged and all can get involved, we need to figure out a national vision for the country. The country needs a purpose and voice and vision,' says Adrian Saville.

None of this is easy: self-interest usually trumps national interest, and few people are able to take a long-term view.

'There is no country that was born rich. Every country that is rich today started poor. And we've got some lovely poster children of quick paths to prosperity: South Korea, Singapore, Estonia, Chile and, more recently, massive progress being made in places like Ethiopia and Rwanda, which are moving quickly up the economic ladder,' says Saville. None of this happens by accident. It all starts with smart, bold policy choices. Moreover, without fail, citizens in those countries put saving first and consumption second.

The fact remains: if you are born on the wrong side of the tracks, the odds are considerably stacked against you. There are many examples of young black South Africans who have managed to improve their economic standing, but they have had to be truly outstanding individuals in order to achieve this. You can be pretty average, but provided you are born into privilege, your odds of success are considerably higher than if you had been born into poverty. In the South African context, our history has ensured that for generations that divide has fallen along racial lines.

The legacy of apartheid and its destructive impact on family life continue to have massive consequences today. Many studies show that living in poverty as a child not only has long-term psychological impacts but health, education and financial consequences too. According to the 2018 South African Child Gauge, carried out by academics at Wits University and UCT, more than six million of the country's children go hungry often and their families cannot provide them with even the minimum amount of nutrition to ensure their healthy development. 'The apartheid regime's deliberate and systematic incursion into family life has meant that the contexts in which children are cared for are often circumscribed by variables beyond the control of the family,' says Child Gauge author Nolwazi Mkhwanazi.

Not only is brain development in those circumstances a serious concern, but environmental factors in poor areas such as noise, substandard housing and family turmoil severely impact on self-confidence, giving rise to the symptom of 'learned helplessness', which can be debilitating if carried through to adulthood.

A study by the non-profit American-based research group Urban Institute found that poverty can have a detrimental impact on a child's ability to succeed at school. According to the study, children who are poor from birth to age two are 30% less likely to complete senior school than children who are poor for the first time later in their life. South African statistics suggest school-dropout rates here are even higher. Absenteeism is higher in poor areas than in wealthier ones, with the added complication that teacher attendance is low at some of the country's more marginal schools.

Scores of international studies show that children who grow up poor have a harder time escaping poverty as adults. A 2009 study by the National Center for Children in Poverty at Columbia University found that children who grew up poor were not only more likely to experience poverty as adults, but that their likelihood of being poor in adulthood increased with the number of years spent in poverty as a child. According to the study, around 5% of adults who never experienced poverty as children were poor at ages 20 and 25. If they spent one to seven years in poverty as a child, that number went up to approximately 13%. For those who spent eight to fourteen years in poverty as children, 46% were poor at age 20, and 40% were poor at age 25.

A growing body of evidence reveals key differences in early brain function between children born in poverty and those in middle-class communities. Researchers at the University of East Anglia studied the brain function of children aged between four months and four years in rural India and found that children from lower-income backgrounds, where mothers also had a low level of education, had weaker brain activity and were more likely to be distracted. It means that they fail to reach their developmental potential. The researchers do provide some hope, however, and suggest that with appropriate interventions, much of the damage can be reversed.

There has been significant progress globally in alleviating poverty. South Africa's carefully considered National Development Plan (NDP), created specifically to address inequality, was launched in 2012. Beyond an initial burst of private-sector enthusiasm and some active marketing by its chief architect, Trevor Manuel, and, since then, some vague platitudes acknowledging its existence, the plan has been gathering dust for most of the time since its publication, through a sheer lack of government interest in actually doing what is required. When Manuel left government, the NDP lost its champion and all its noble, achievable ideals were effectively lost. There is plenty of good reason for the current administration to reconvene the brains trust that drew up the document, review it and relaunch it.

While South Africa was caught up in the state-capture project, much of the rest of the world actually managed to attain the first Millennium Development Goals target, to cut the 1990 poverty rate in half by 2015. This was achieved in 2010, five years ahead of schedule.

While large parts of the world have made great progress in this respect, more than half the world's extreme poor live in sub-Saharan Africa, where the number of people living in poverty has increased. If that trend continues, by 2030 nearly nine out of ten extremely poor people in the world will be in sub-Saharan Africa. That is our problem, and it is not a crisis we want to have to manage later.

Although the vicious cycle of being born in poverty, remaining in poverty and passing poverty on to one's children seems cast in iron, the one thing that can help break the cycle is education. For failure in adulthood is not a foregone conclusion to those born in poverty, just as financial success is not guaranteed to those born in privileged circumstances.

CHAPTER 6
. . . .

Education

'The best way to predict the future is to create it.'
– Abraham Lincoln

There is widespread agreement that South Africa's public education system is failing the country's young people. This is despite
the fact that in 2019, for example, R262.4bn was allocated by
the government to school-level education – about 16% of the total national budget. It's the single biggest allocation to any state
activity in South Africa, and it shows that the government understands the importance of education as one of the fundamental
building blocks of the economy. Yet the country's primary education system is rated in the World Economic Forum's *Global
Competitiveness Report* as one of the worst in the world. It has
been for years. The Department of Education can massage the
data any way it pleases, but the brutal reality remains that South
Africa's publicly educated young people barely stand a chance in
a globally competitive jobs market, unless the education system
becomes fit for the future rather than a self-congratulatory soap
opera once a year.

As mentioned earlier, the 2016 PIRLS showed that 78% of Grade 4 students in South Africa could not read for meaning. The figure was even higher when children were tested in languages other than English and Afrikaans. This makes South Africa unique among upper-middle-income countries. More than half of the children in its public schools don't understand the meaning of the words on the page in front of them. South Africa came last out of 50 countries surveyed.

Educationists point out that one of the biggest problems in the South African education system is that children in the intermediate phase of learning are pushed into an English language curriculum, which adversely affects their cognitive skills and constrains development later. Studies have shown that children whose early learning is conducted in their mother tongue perform better when learning is transferred to English later in their school careers.

South Africa has to deal with primary education urgently. Lobby groups like the NGO Equal Education have long pointed out that government over-invests in educating pupils in their final year of school, despite scientific evidence that the money to develop real learning is better spent in the formative years. There is too great an obsession with matric. Moreover, the fact that only half the children who enrol in primary school in year one make it to the examination table by the end of year 12 is an indictment of the system. Pass rates are inflated by virtue of the fact that the requirements are embarrassingly low. In addition, most children in public schools have to cope with overcrowded classrooms, and inadequately trained and poorly supported teachers. The real test lies in the teenager's preparedness for tertiary education. Only a tiny number are able to enter the tertiary sector with any degree of confidence that they will achieve degrees or diplomas within the stipulated course times. Again, it is those with the solid grounding, more often than not from privileged backgrounds, who have the highest chance of success. South Africa's genetic lottery still plays a critical role in determining the outcomes.

Nic Spaull, senior researcher in education at Stellenbosch University, says South Africa's income inequalities are exactly mirrored in the education system, where more than three-quarters of schools are largely dysfunctional. This immediately puts children who are subjected to substandard education at a disadvantage for life. How do you give hope to a generation of young people, most of whom are failed by the education system? They have no discernible skills, no decent qualification to enable them to enter gainful employment. They are therefore doomed to fall between the cracks and have a very high chance of joining the 10 million or so people of working age who cannot find work, even if they wanted to.

This is South Africa's biggest single crisis and it is the issue that leads to high levels of hopelessness, which translates eventually into frustration and anger. South Africa's failed education system renders young people unemployable.

Biscuit entrepreneur Simon Mantell, writing in the *Daily Maverick*, commented that despite the constitutional guarantee affirming the right of young South Africans to obtain a proper education and despite the vast amount of money thrown at the problem, outcomes are so poor that most young people emerge at the other side of the system ill equipped to contribute productively to the economy. Far too many people get to the end of 12 years of schooling functionally illiterate, innumerate, and with little or no cognitive ability.

'The continued failure of our school system means most of our youth face a life sentence of menial, hard and unskilled labour at low hourly rates in the unlikely event they ever find permanent employment ... For 25 years the governing party and its alliance partners have refused to grasp the stinging nettle that the first building block of true black economic empowerment is a world-class education. Rather than deliver on this constitutional requirement, the government has preferred to distract masses with pie-in-the-sky job creation promises, together with pledges of decent work at decent pay. The terrible truth for school leavers from the "township" schools and many tertiary institutions is that they are, in a word, unemployable.' It's a harsh reality that, if South Africa does not face it, will be its downfall. According to Stats SA, 99% of children in the country aged 7–15 are enrolled in school, but just how many of them are being treated with the basic respect that accompanies decent tuition?

'Given the obvious and disastrous education deficit, the relevant question becomes: is it possible for an employer to offer employment other than the most mundane of tasks and, if so, can the potential employee's total lack of educational foundation allow for significant training or upskilling, leading to improved productivity, greater responsibilities, better remuneration and the promised "better life for all"? The short answer is that employers don't have the capacity or time to provide what is essentially primary and secondary education to potential employees and will rather automate or deindustrialise, as evidenced in South Africa over the last 15 years.'

This explains why South Africa falls short in so many global surveys on competitiveness. It also goes a long way to explaining South Africa's inequality crisis. If you are born poor and black in this country, you are likely, barring divine intervention, to die under similar circumstances. Moreover, future generations of your family will remain starved of capital and unable to create the inter-generational wealth that gives those born into wealthier homes an advantage from the moment of birth. For it is the financial circumstances of parents that have a greater impact on whether a child thrives in the schooling system than the individual ability of the child itself.

While access to education has improved over the past two and a half decades, the poor quality of what government provides seriously undermines the prospect of young people thriving in an increasingly competitive world. With the looming risk that low-skill jobs will be performed increasingly by technology, job prospects for young people with poor critical thinking and analytical skills are seriously under threat.

The inequality of the system is amplified by the education outcomes. For example, just 3% of South Africa's schools produce 98% of matric mathematics distinctions. That's not because the best students attend a minority of schools, but it suggests that resources and teaching methods are inadequate to meet the potential of young people.

You cannot have a fully functioning and globally competitive economy if you are not providing it with the skills it needs to grow. Consistently poor education standards are a severe brake on growth. Companies searching for skills look at the talent pool and government's local hiring requirements, and find that the low skills base alongside tortuous government bureaucracy and restrictive labour regulations is a serious constraint when it comes to new investment.

There are many ways of effecting education. You don't need to build a school or devise a new way of delivering education to do it. Sometimes it's as simple as supporting those who are already doing it.

Louise van Rhyn started the NGO Partners for Possibility in 2010, creating a mechanism whereby private-sector executives would adopt a school and work with the head teacher to improve the management and administration of the institution. The lessons have been extraordinary. About a thousand under-resourced government schools have been reached and as a result, by applying business principles of team-building, inspiring staff and getting parents more engaged with their children's education, about 880,000 children have benefited from the programme.

It turns out that the learning has been reciprocal. By becoming intimately involved in the trials and tribulations of under-resourced schools, business leaders have been forced to leave the ivory towers of their executive office spaces and immerse themselves in the often-brutal reality of what it is like to be poor and marginalised in society.

As the *Business Insider South Africa* editor Helena Wasserman observed on taking her child to a provincial chess tournament

in the Western Cape, where she saw the chasm of inequality between privileged and underprivileged schools demolished by the
skills shown by the poorer children: 'Game after game, these
children, who during breaks practised their moves on cheap, min-
iature chess sets carefully positioned on toilet paper to protect
them from the grass, came out on top. At the end of the weekend,
township school teams were ranked first in four of the six primary
school age categories. Seeing these kids – many of them girls – in
their torn jerseys, calmly demolishing their opponents was one
of those lump-in-the-throat moments all South Africans know
so well. This is what happens when the playing field is level-ish.
Apart from the expensive experts who coach the higher-income
schools, for once having money wasn't going to set you apart.
To be great at chess, you don't need an astro-turf playing field,
a multi-million-rand science centre, a digitised school library, or
math teachers who have actuarial degrees. You need intellectual
stamina, grit and the hunger to practise for hours. Even if you
come from a poor school that has been starved of resources and
neglected for decades and where children die in pit latrines – even
amid poverty and daily crime, you can be excellent at chess.'

This story epitomises what Partners for Possibility stands for.

Entrepreneur Gill Cox runs Numatics SA, a family-owned
industrial-automation business, with her husband in KZN. She
was teamed with Bizie Magwaza, who was catapulted into the head
teacher role without any real preparation at Mshwati Memorial
Primary School in Upper Tongaat. The school, like many rural institutions, had high rates of pupil absenteeism. The Grade R class
was seeing an average of 12 days of absenteeism every term.

The school enlisted the support of Ian Wilson, who runs the Ride and Glide mountain biking programme, to encourage attendance. Children with a 100% attendance record each week were allowed to participate in Friday cycling sessions. Ian nearly gave up, but word spread and soon absenteeism rates dropped; within three years there was virtually no absenteeism. His involvement led to a feeding programme, too. Wilson saw that many of the children were arriving at school without having had anything to eat in the morning. In the year in which the feeding programme was introduced, the entire Grade R group passed into Grade 1 on merit. Not a single child was 'progressed' to the next grade.

Mshwati became a community project, drawing on the cooperation of teachers at Ashton private school in Ballito. When it emerged that many of the problems the Mshwati children were having could be resolved through different teaching methods, Ashton's teachers created videos that were distributed via WhatsApp to their colleagues at Mshwati. At the end of two years the school, led by its principal, with the support of the community, had become a fundamentally different, productive place.

Another of the Partners for Possibility interventions brought FirstRand executive Clive Naicker into partnership with Dalton Ramaoma, the principal of David Makhubo Secondary School at Kaalfontein in Midrand. 'How hard could it be?' Clive thought to himself as he volunteered his services. At work he was managing big teams and big budgets on a daily basis. He knew his stuff. But he was not really prepared for what became a life-changing experience.

'I feel like I belong to society now; before, I felt isolated. I feel more socially accepted, I am better able to handle conflict, get people to deliver and ensure that I communicate in a way that my message gets across. I am better able to understand people and work better with them; it's not just about me, it's about the team.'

Clive arrived without any of the trappings of power and influence that he enjoyed at FirstRand. He found an ambitious headmaster constrained by budgets and a lack of formal management training. He found, too, that he had to work hard to earn not only the respect of the teachers but their trust too. Clive maintains that he learned more at the school about leadership and management than he did in the confines of his MBA class.

One of the frustrations of high-powered executives working in large corporates is that they are invariably a small cog in a huge machine; it is often difficult for them to measure the actual impact they have in their organisations. By involving themselves in struggling schools, they can see the positive impact they can make as they assist motivated head teachers to develop and help grow the institutions entrusted to them.

Nedbank executive Grant Kelly was partnered with the principal of Summat College in Pretoria, Freddy Antwi. The school's academic performance was good, which meant they were able to focus on other longer-term goals, such as reforming an antiquated and punitive disciplinary regime. By doing so, they reduced other incidents of violence at the school as children learned to deal with conflict differently. 'It required a mindset shift, away from providing answers and towards supporting my partner in his attempts to address issues,' Kelly says.

There are scores of similar case studies from the Partners for Possibility programme. Each is remarkable. The model of providing support for head teachers to empower them to better manage schools has had a marked impact on the results and education levels of the children. It's proven. And it needs state backing to achieve scale. Just some of the billions thrown at public education in this country in the hope that it will land in the right place could be reallocated and applied to change children's lives.

Money is not the problem. Rather, poor management of schools and of teaching staff is clearly a significant brake on progress. Other problems are poor teaching and a curriculum that is increasingly inadequate for the task of turning out globally competitive talent in a world where children of the same age elsewhere are being taught to withstand the threat of competition from other parts of the world and the great unknown danger of rapidly advancing technology.

Without radical intervention in our schools, the future is bleak. If failure is a result of bad choices, then it's logical that success is achieved through making good choices. A failure is simply a problem looking for a solution. And that problem, in the right hands, can be a significant opportunity.

'I believe it's up to us as citizens of the country to create the change. We actually don't have time to wait for government to improve the status quo,' says Stacey Brewer, who has built up SPARK Schools. SPARK is a private-schools business funded by a mix of angel and venture-capital investors who like the approach that she and co-founder Ryan Harrison took to building their business in education, from scratch.

The pair started out with the fundamental belief that they could revolutionise, at scale, the way education is run in South Africa and could develop a business model which they could export to other countries. 'We see our children perform two to three years behind what is needed, but by using blended learning we are able to quickly catch them up to global standards,' Brewer says. Blended learning makes use of a mix of technology and classroom education. Children achieve higher education outcomes than those in regular government schools, and the results far outstrip those provided by the public sector, at a price that is comparable to what government spends per child. The quality is derived from the use of data analytics, which enables teachers to provide differentiated instruction in the class and in IT labs. The technology identifies which children are struggling, thereby allowing for more intense focus by the teacher and enabling kids who are working quickly and accurately to be stretched and to enhance their performance. It also allows for extension, review and reinforcement of learned material.

Brewer is not reinventing education. That is not necessary. There is no magic wand to solve the problems that the public system faces. What she has done is to take some of the best available technology in the world and not only adapt it, but also apply it locally, in a highly effective and systematised fashion, which allows the programme to be replicated across multiple campuses. Its power lies in the data analytics, which determines how teaching is applied in practical terms to ensure that each child is given optimal, individualised education. It is designed to develop critical-thinking skills, and the results show that it is working.

Textbooks, the annual bugbear of the Department of Education, which spends a fortune on procuring and distributing them, are not part of the SPARK model. Technology is kept secure at school, and the learning is done there. Children do not take devices home. This makes for a higher level of security in respect of the equipment, which is owned, managed and maintained by the company.

The focus of SPARK is on delivering the South African education curriculum but doing it at a globally competitive standard. While Grade 1s in South Africa are expected to be able to count only to ten, the SPARK application of the curriculum has them counting at least up to 100 by the end of the first formal year of schooling. The attitude is that the children are perfectly capable of doing so, and so rather than restricting the ability of bright young minds, they are stretched beyond the narrow confines and low expectations of the national curriculum.

No child gets left behind, thanks to the technology-driven analysis of their performance, and none slips through the cracks. We all know of bright young kids who either missed the point of pi or Pythagoras and, rather than seek help in the class, quietly disappeared into the background; by the time they were tested at the end of term, for many it was too late to catch up.

Brewer admits that in the start-up phase she and her team were 'cowboys' figuring out how best to apply the theory of the MBA thesis she had submitted on blended learning and that they were now looking to leverage in the real world. Like all start-ups, they were idea-rich and cash-poor. They had no market credibility. While her business partner had worked in IT in the UK, Brewer herself had no corporate experience beyond working in hospitality. Neither had an idea of how to structure a business, and they were running around raising money, recruiting staff, and convincing families that they had a new, credible way of delivering education to young minds and should be trusted to do so.

'I didn't have anything to lose. Right from the beginning, I was very fortunate to have a lot of supporters and mentors to keep it going. I'd never had corporate experience and in many ways that has been good because I have not been conditioned in any particular way.'

Growing a new business requires tenacity, grit and a constant desire to do better. By her own admission, Brewer is tough to please and is always seeking new ways of improving the process of delivering education. That can cause discomfort among staff, who can struggle to keep up with the rapid pace of change. After opening 21 schools by the start of 2019, Brewer was encouraged by her board and investors to pause and consolidate the rapid gains she and her staff had made. She hired a finance professional, the company's first chief financial officer, to formalise processes and systems, and give the firm a chance to breathe a little before embarking on the next phase of growth.

Suddenly there is plenty to lose. The founders have committed six of the most productive years of their lives to a project which has become a substantial business, educating nearly 15,000 children and employing more than 1,000 staff – a large number of people for whose well-being they are responsible. They have funders to keep happy and high levels of parent expectation. There is a huge amount at stake. And that makes for a perfect balance of incentives. If parents decide they can get better value for their money elsewhere, they will move their children to another place that better suits them and their budgets.

By 2023, their tenth anniversary, SPARK aims to have 65 schools in operation. It's a monumental ambition, considering that the first school opened in Randburg in 2013 and the second one started only two years later. But Brewer continues to surprise herself with what is possible through an unwavering focus and the ability to outsource to others the work of setting up new campuses. 'If your dreams don't scare you, they are not big enough,' says Brewer. 'I love challenges. I love being uncomfortable.'

Government is paying attention to what SPARK is doing. The blended-learning model is being tested in pilot projects in the Western Cape. Brewer is open to partnerships. She would happily run schools for government on a budget. Such an arrangement happens in the US, and charter schools in the UK are joint ventures too, where they are publicly funded and privately run.

Government has been slow to take up the private sector offers of assistance. This was the lesson learned by Chris van der Merwe, the founder of the Curro schools empire, when he pointed out to government that he was able to build schools to state specifications faster and with better quality, all within budget, than the government was doing itself. A 1,500-pupil school can cost R120m to build and R30m a year to run. Government is yet to take up the offer of assistance. In the meantime, the chasm between what government is able to deliver and what is achieved in the private sector is marked.

With just four schools and a desperate need for funding in 2009, Van der Merwe went to pitch his idea to the board of PSG. As we have seen, then chairman Jannie Mouton was won over halfway through Van der Merwe's pitch. PSG bought its initial 50% stake in Curro in 2009 for just R50m, and paid as much a year later for a further 26% through Paladin Capital. The firm has raised about R3bn through rights issues in expanding, and today has a market value of R8bn and trades at a multiple of 32 times the previous year's profit.

The PSG investment came as the worst global economic crisis since the Great Depression struck. Businesses were shutting down; shops were closing; banks were failing globally. But Curro was addressing a deep-seated need in the minds of South African consumers. The firm now operates more than 110 schools on 80 campuses and has its own teacher-training college. It educates more than 40,000 youngsters a year, and the number is growing.

Before his retirement due to ill health, Mouton, whose early interest provided the impetus for growth, urged the firm to target 500 schools by 2030. But that goal will need to be flexible considering the slowdown in the economy as well as reports from private-education businesses that demand for their offering has dropped along with a rise in middle-class emigration. But the group has been building up stocks of land to ensure it can meet its goals, and owns more than 150 plots for future expansion.

Curro nearly lost focus about five years ago when it tried, and failed, to buy ADvTECH, the listed owner of Crawford College and other education brands. The offer was rebuffed amid a rebellion by parents concerned that it would concentrate too much power in the hands of a single company. The firm has since redoubled its efforts to grow while splitting off its tertiary business into a new listed company called Stadio. Van der Merwe left Curro to establish the new start-up.

The rise of private education has grown since 1994, in much the same way as private health care has evolved amid the growing burden on the state and its failure to deliver adequate levels of service. Today about 5% of South African children are educated privately. The vacuum left by state failure has led to the creation of substantial private-school businesses, and government should be able to embrace the opportunity to learn from their successes. Education, including the demand for new schools, puts a big burden on the state. The Public Investment Corporation owns a small stake in Curro. The state could raise capital by selling land to Curro and, through a raised equity investment, plough the dividends into public education. Properly managed, it could be a win-win arrangement. 'We would love to be more involved with government, and it would mean that we would be able to reach many more communities. It really could change the country and its prospects,' says Stacey Brewer.

Government could also rethink its funding model, and thereby contribute to greater choice for families. Imagine if, instead of blindly funding an education system, government funded each child and gave parents the choice as to where they sent their children to school and provided schools with the freedom to charge what they wanted for education. The children would be required to present the voucher for access to school, and that voucher would only be made available if their parent or guardian had a tax number, regardless of whether they were obliged to file a return or not. This would enable the best-managed schools to grow with a subsidy.

A good government school, with a capable head teacher and motivated staff, might be able to charge R3,000 a month as opposed to the standard government funding of about R2,000 a child, and it could use the extra money to improve services and facilities, perhaps even pay their best teachers a little more. It would create an incentive for educators to perform and a more competitive environment. Some schools would still fail, but if you create the right incentives, a greater number should do better, leaving fewer schools that require direct government intervention.

If you chose to educate your child at an R8,000-a-month elite school, you would also receive a subsidy funded by the taxes you pay. SARS would then be able to cross-reference its taxpayer database with the education vouchers used at different schools and might be better able to pinpoint which families were dodging the tax net.

Such a system would also create an incentive for the likes of SPARK Schools and other privately funded institutions to develop more quickly because parents would be able to make a choice of school rather than simply consigning their child to the nearest institution in the hope that they might learn something.

If you turn up at any SPARK school first thing in the morning, you will observe a school assembly such as you have never experienced before. If you were born in the 1970s and went to a government school, you might recall the stiff formality of sitting on hard concrete or on the cold tarmac of the school quad with your legs crossed and your back up straight and being admonished by a severe head teacher, followed perhaps by a hellfire-and-brimstone Bible reading and the singing of the school song, if you had one, or the national anthem, before you began your day of rote learning under the perpetual threat of corporal punishment.

A SPARK Schools assembly looks to the untrained eye like every 1970s educator's idea of hell. The children enjoy themselves. They sing. They dance. They laugh. They are motivated to think beyond the narrow confines of the school room. Each teacher takes a turn. Armed only with a microphone, a strong presence and the promise of endorphins, the teacher on duty on the morning I attend belts out:

'SPARK Bramley, are you ready!'

'Ready!'

'SPARK Bramley, are you ready!'

'Ready!'

'Boogie, boogie, ay, boogie ay-ya-ya!'

To which the children reply: 'Boogie, boogie, ay, boogie ay-ya-ya!'

This is repeated, whispered, shouted and whispered again. The children are fully engaged.

'Today is a Wednesday! Who can tell me the date?'

Little hands shoot up.

Many answers are wrong. But they are in the zone.

The PA system blasts out a backing track. The kids sing along to a pop song about growing and climbing mountains and achieving greatness. Not everyone knows the words, but they are singing along as if it's the only thing that matters in the world. Teachers better have rhythm. They are keeping time and looking out for kids who are letting their enthusiasm get the better of them.

'Sit!'

'Stand up!'

'Strike a pose!' instructs the teacher. It's not clear at this point who is having more fun, the staff or the children.

Another song starts. Kids start bopping to the rhythm. Teachers are dancing. The kids are getting rid of nervous energy, enabling them, when they get to class, to focus on the day ahead.

One more chant before school time.

'What are you going to do?' asks the teacher into the microphone.

'We are going to university!' comes back the chant.

'What?'

'We're going to go to university!'

And even if they don't go to university one day, they are being given the very best possible shot at it.

. . . .

CHAPTER 7

Learning from billionaires

'Pointing fingers, however valid, isn't always productive.
Get involved. Start something.' – Michael Jordaan

Have you ever wondered why some people succeed and others don't? Why some lives are more remarkable than others? It's tempting in South Africa to assume that success stems from a privileged past. Having a head start doesn't hurt, but it's by no means a guarantee of success.

There's lots of literature on the subject and you will learn all kinds of fascinating theories about success in books by authors such as Malcolm Gladwell, who has made a living out of turning dry academic theory into lively, meaningful prose, and the collaborative work of Steven Levitt and Stephen Dubner, one an economist and the other a storyteller.

After studying entrepreneurs for more than two decades, I have come to the conclusion that it's about considerably more than education, aptitude or blind luck. All those things are important, but that's too simplistic. It also helps if you are born into a family that is not worried about where the next meal is coming from or whether there will be money for university fees. It helps where you are born, to whom, and how and where you were educated, but even among the lofty elite only a small handful of individuals create anything brand-new and meaningful. Many of their peers are successful surgeons, bank managers or lawyers, but few develop their abilities into ideas that change the world.

So much of the success of entrepreneurs comes down to mindset: the ability to see a problem as a challenge to be solved rather than as a barrier to success. Also, not one of a dozen or so entrepreneurs I spoke to for this book ever started out on their venture for the sake of the money. Not one of them ever expected they would accumulate the extraordinary wealth their work has brought them. That was not ever their primary objective. They all wanted success and to be recognised for their efforts, but money was not the driving force.

It's blindingly obvious, but needs to be said: every business that has ever existed was once a small business. Why did Bidvest flourish or Aspen Pharmacare or FirstRand or Discovery, while thousands of others failed? What made Christo Wiese into one of the most extraordinary entrepreneurs the country has seen in the past half-century – and was there anything in his character that contributed to his losing most of his fortune in a matter of a week in 2017 when Steinhoff, once the sixth most valuable company on the JSE, succumbed to South Africa's biggest corporate fraud to date?

Think back to your schooldays. Who were the whizz-kids? Some have no doubt done well. They may be senior executives in large companies, doctors or lawyers. But who stands out today, and did you see that star quality in them in their teenage years? How many have crashed and burned? How many are just getting by? How many are dead as a result of the stress they have put themselves under in their quest to live up to that early promise?

Banker turned venture capitalist Michael Jordaan remembers that Elon Musk was in pre-school with him in Pretoria. He can't recall whether the South African-born creator of PayPal, Tesla and SpaceX was obviously destined to be a superstar back then. Some kids flourish later than others; some not at all. Who would have thought my old classmate James Fisher, a quiet, diligent but unassuming kid, would be the guy who invented the snakeboard and would become one of South Africa's biggest shipbuilders? Others closer to him may have seen his prowess, but I don't recall him hustling in the playground. Brett Kebble, on the other hand, always hustled – but that was another school and his habits, learned early, led him to a messy end.

A recent report by UBS and PwC found that there are three primary character traits that billionaires share:

- smart risk-taking
- focus
- long-term thinking.

Intelligence isn't at the top of the list. One study by German researcher Rainer Zitelmann, who wrote the book *The Wealth Elite*, found that super-wealthy entrepreneurs had higher tolerances for frustration and were more detail-oriented than most people. That ability to cope with frustration, particularly in a place like South Africa where it's practically impossible to operate with any degree of certainty about critical issues of policy, currency and economic stability, is a crucial asset.

Zitelmann has said, according to *Business Insider*: 'To sum this up, you can say that rich people are less neurotic and less agreeable, but have a higher degree of conscientiousness, are more open to new experiences and more extroverted than the population as a whole.'

They tend also to be nonconformists, who demonstrate individuality at an early age, and also rule-breakers. Think of the likes of Steve Jobs and Richard Branson. Interestingly, these are the sorts of characteristics that could also be applied to white-collar criminals. For many, they could have gone either way. As for those who stick to the straight and narrow, they are able to create immense value.

The 2019 *Billionaire Report* suggests that companies run by billionaires perform twice as well as the rest of the market. It's an American study, but much of what it says holds true for South Africa where many of today's billionaires who started out 30 to 40 years ago certainly exhibited those characteristics. There are a multitude of books and studies which illustrate that billionaires think differently from the rest of us.

In my research for this book I asked about a dozen founders of large South African companies what had made them successful. They had several things in common. They were by nature optimists. They were incredibly smart. They were well versed in the art of decision-making. They were able to park emotion when it came to making big calls. They had a growth mindset, and possessed an uncanny ability to look through political and social noise and focus on the task at hand. All this correlates nicely with international research, except that in South Africa successful leaders have needed a cast-iron constitution when it comes to dealing with political risk and the consequences of state failure.

Here are some of their stories from which current and even future generations of leaders might just learn.

For Raymond Ackerman, fired from his job as MD of Checkers in 1966 at the age of 35, it was always about humility. Not long before he was dismissed for refusing a board instruction to expand margins and fix the prices of consumer goods, a young man called Jack Goldin had phoned him from Cape Town telling him about a small chain he had started called Pick n Pay.

Says Ackerman, 'I invited him to come and see me, and on the day he arrived I cleared my diary and went to meet him at the airport. American supermarket operators had always been kind to me when I was developing Checkers, so I showed him around, and it's a lesson that has always stuck with me. When I got fired I got a call from Jack, who told me he wanted to sell and he could think of no one better suited to take over his business than me. All because I took the time and I showed him around. Call it luck if you want, but I made time for him even though I was running 82 stores, and that meeting with him changed my life.'

Ackerman didn't have the money that Goldin asked for the chain of four stores, so he took contributions, in the style of many start-ups, from friends, fools and family. After starting negotiations at R580,000, Goldin pushed him to R600,000 and eventually late that night to R620,000. Ackerman agreed, going

against the advice of his brother-in-law, who kicked his ankle so
hard under the table that he says it still aches in Cape Town's
cold, wet winters. The deal was sealed and the Ackerman family
relocated to Cape Town to build the business. 'My biggest lesson
is that you should never get too big for your boots,' Ackerman
says. That's old school for 'don't be arrogant'.

Ackerman has a few regrets. One is that he trusted too much
and didn't fire fast enough. There were several cases in his career when he placed loyalty above business sense and didn't get
rid of people quickly enough. He declined to name names. He
also allowed himself to be distracted by two failed forays into
Australia, the graveyard of many South African corporate ambitions. While he was focusing his energies on trying to get those
businesses working Down Under, he was losing traction in his
home market and allowed a gap for the growth of Shoprite and
Checkers, which rather than squandering capital on international
misadventures were building their capacity at home.

Pick n Pay was South Africa's top-end grocer in its heyday.
When SAB decided it should divest from the debt-laden OK
Bazaars, Ackerman declined the opportunity to buy it. It was on
the market for R1 and the buyer would have to assume the R200m
debt – a lot of money, especially back then. Ackerman's eye was
elsewhere when Whitey Basson went to see his chairman, Christo
Wiese, and asked him if they should buy the business. Wiese re-
calls counselling Basson that if he did not buy it and Ackerman
did, then he would have a fight on his hands at the lower end
of the grocery market. It would make far greater sense for him
to consolidate his hold on serving South Africa's lower-income

segment than leave a gap for Ackerman to bring the fight to him. Basson pounced, and the business became cash-positive in less time than it takes to have a baby. Basson has subsequently taken the Checkers brand to compete head-on with Pick n Pay, and some analysts suggest it is winning the battle.

How, I asked Laurie Dippenaar, one of three co-founders of the R450bn banking and insurance giant FirstRand, did the relationship between three headstrong, capable, independent-minded individuals function? Few people can make partnerships work. It has to be more difficult when there are three people who need to collaborate to achieve the best possible outcome for their shared project.

'Facts,' he said.

'Elaborate,' I countered.

'We only ever debated the merits of a decision based on facts, and whoever argued the facts best carried the day. If you have facts that you base your decision on to make your case, it's far more effective than just being the smooth-talking salesman. You can over-analyse and never get to a decision. There is no such thing as the perfect decision. You have to get the best minds around the table, make a decision and put foot.'

'We' in this context are Dippenaar, GT Ferreira and Paul Harris. The initial triumvirate included Eastern Cape businessman Pat Goss, but he left what was in its early stage the corporate-finance company Rand Consolidated Investments (RCI) to run the family business of Jumbo Cash and Carry after his father died. Dippenaar and Ferreira then brought in Harris. Goss got to keep his shares in the original business and has added to his holdings over his lifetime, making him independently wealthy even though he didn't ever work as an executive in the business.

There was an acceptance at FirstRand that even with the smartest people available to debate just the facts, mistakes would be made, but they also saw no value in waiting for the perfect environment in which to reach a weighty decision. There will always be pros and cons. The job of decision-makers – and the reason they are paid more than their peers – is that they have to weigh up the choices open to an organisation, and make the best possible decision in the circumstances at that moment and then act on that decision. There can be no result if a decision is not acted upon. If it transpires that the choice made was the wrong one, there is no shame in changing direction. Rather that than keep at a bad idea and execute it in a half-hearted fashion, if the project is doomed.

The FirstRand story, like many others, resonates with Robert Shiller's theory that the world is shaped around the stories we choose to tell.

'I don't believe we have had chaos. Chaos is Syria,' says Dippenaar, who is well known for his ability to distil massive complexity into easy-to-understand anecdotes. (He could have used Venezuela or even Zimbabwe to make his point. But at the time of our discussion, Syria was making headlines, so it was a logical choice.) For those who refuse to get mired in the negativity of the Sunday afternoon braai discussion, being able to drill through the noise and focus on facts is an extraordinary attribute and is part of the reason why massively successful business leaders over the past four decades have been able to capitalise on the myriad opportunities available to those willing to take risks in what most perceive as a hostile environment.

'Bidvest does not participate in any recession.' This slogan, which features on the posters in each and every Bidvest facility in the world, speaks about mindset. Of course, Bidvest has to do business in a difficult environment just like every other corporation, but it chooses to approach the obstacles in its way with a problem-solving mindset in the knowledge that its competitors are likely to get caught up in the negativity, while it focuses on the opportunities.

For the founder, Brian Joffe, a chartered accountant, who learned his trade at the feet of another legendary entrepreneur by the name of Manny Simchowitz, timing was important. He laid the groundwork for Bidvest in the messy debris of the South African economy after PW Botha's Rubicon speech, which pushed South Africa so deep into junk that it couldn't see any hope of ever recovering. It was a terrible time to start a business. Indeed, if you look at a graph of the South African economy over the past four decades, there have been very few periods not mired in crisis and high levels of volatility.

'I started then, because that's when I was ready to start, there was an opportunity in 1988 and 1989, institutions needed an outlet for their money and enabled people like myself to have a quick start and get on with it,' says Joffe, who retired from Bidvest to focus on a new listing in his eighth decade called Long4Life (it's proving a lot harder the second time around). 'Being a white guy at that time and being part of a system that allowed you to do whatever you wanted, there were no competition rules, there was no red tape, we were lucky. All of us can go back in time and say it was tough, but it was easy times too because if it was today, I challenge any of the people you are talking to, to say it's just as easy today to start something new. Because it's not. It's much more difficult today.'

Discovery, when it was started by Adrian Gore, had one big goal – to use behavioural economics to reform medical insurance by putting the onus on the patient to live better and claim more sparingly through a complex series of incentives. Gore's idea had been rejected by Liberty, his employer, where he worked as an actuary, so he went across town to meet a man who had a reputation for backing good entrepreneurs.

'Where's your product?' Gore remembers Laurie Dippenaar asking. 'Where's your team?'

Gore had neither, so he was offered a desk in exchange for control of the company and was told to get on with creating a business. It took him six months to tick off the first thing on his 'to-do' list, which still hangs in his home office today – his instruction to himself: 'Hire an actuary.' So he appointed Herschel Mayers, and the two set about creating a diversified financial-services company in what might have been regarded by others as a saturated market. They started in health insurance and gradually diversified into other products, most recently into banking.

Why would you go into banking when there was just so much political noise around banks and banking? The Reserve Bank was under siege amid a long-running effort to have it nationalised, and commercial banks too were coming under significant pressure. Why would anyone invest north of R7.5bn in a brand-new bank in an environment seemingly intent on reducing competition rather than allowing it to flourish?

'If it's not Armageddon, you must be building. It's an obvious conclusion. If people are worried, prices of opportunities are typically undervalued, so if you can you should either be building or buying. That strategy doesn't work only if there is Armageddon; but if there isn't, you will always be better off,' Gore tells me. 'Take the road less travelled: I tell my kids this all the time. You're not going to make it if you follow others. It's so hard. But how can you be successful if you follow what everyone else is doing? By definition, success is delta to the mean.'

Discovery has been built over more than 25 years. There have been no big bets that could have collapsed the entire edifice. There was a moment when they thought they could take on the American establishment but, after investing R1bn in Destiny Health, pulled the plug on the project. It was not a failure, insists Gore, but rather a lesson in decision-making and about how not to throw good money after bad. Gore's natural style is considered consensus-making. Nothing happens quickly. That way there are no big, irrecoverable disasters.

Gore never takes anything at face value. If anything, he is a definite contrarian and does not accept dogma. The moment he is told something is an inflexible absolute, he is prone to challenge it. 'I do like complexity. I do like seeing this in a far more profound sense, it's my natural curiosity. But I like a complex business. My natural paranoia is building a business where barriers to entry are high. Hiring the smartest people and using the smartest systems, where you deal with something the average company cannot deal with, gives me a sense of comfort. I like complex thinking. It's my natural desire, so I guess I have come to learn that you take something complex but make it intuitive. It must be simple to the user, but it must be underpinned by complexity. I would feel very vulnerable selling widgets,' says Gore by way of explaining how he keeps competitors from muscling in on his turf.

An interesting test case is playing out in South Africa's courts right now, in which Liberty, Gore's old employer, invited its clients to provide proof of their Vitality status, an offering created by Discovery to help it better understand the risk profile of its clientele. On discovering whether its own clients were on Bronze, Silver, Gold or Diamond, Liberty would then structure its own product incentives, using a rival's offering. Liberty argues that the data used to create the status belongs to the client and not Discovery. It will be an interesting battle. Vitality underpins all of Discovery's global offerings, and has become a product sold to more than 20 international operations around the world.

It's a fallacy to think that today's billionaires planned every detail of their success, Christo Wiese told me less than a week before most of his fortune evaporated amid the collapse of Steinhoff. 'When a small-business person looks at a so-called big-business person, he thinks to himself, you know, that guy must have had a wonderful blueprint. Because otherwise, how could it all have developed so nicely? The truth is that business is all about opportunistic moves. It's all opportunistically driven, not blueprint-driven. So there was no grand plan. If someone tells you that they knew 50 years ago that one day they would be a group with more than 20,000 shops spread all over the world, in 30-plus countries employing 300,000 people, with different languages, different cultures – who could foresee that? If somebody tells you that he had developed such a plan 50 years ago, he's a liar.'

I cannot tell you how many times I have watched the 47-minute video I shot of Wiese on my phone. At that moment his world was collapsing around him. He'd not yet come to the final realisation that Markus Jooste, his trusted lieutenant, would soon stop returning his calls and issue his mea culpa apologising for 'mistakes' and accepting responsibility for the imminent collapse of Steinhoff. PwC would later uncover the details of South Africa's biggest corporate fraud of R105bn. Looking at Wiese and his responses to my questions about the multinational retailer he and Jooste were then building, I can see no obvious signs of distress. Either he was a consummate poker player or he had no idea about the catastrophe that was about to envelop his empire.

'To be an entrepreneur you have to be quite mad,' he said without a hint of irony. 'There is so much in the world that is beyond your control that can and will go wrong. What if Kim and Trump fire nuclear rockets at each other? If your personality is such that you focus on all those things that can go wrong, you will never get started.'

Stephen Koseff of Investec and his business collaborator of 40 years, Bernard Kantor, retired from the group at the end of 2018. Koseff remains an active voice for a greater role for business in helping get South Africa back on track. Investec built a reputation for itself as being a risk-taker. 'We'd break china for the client,' Koseff said with specific reference to the deal that gave

Aspen Pharmacare the scale it needed to become a global player. 'We sat with those guys through the night to do a deal.' Stephen Saad, the founder of Aspen, has dined out on the story for years that part of the deal was that the firm would sell off the factories it had bought. When Saad saw the factories and realised they were world-class facilities, he reneged on that aspect of the deal, much to the fury of Investec at the time. It was the right thing to do. Billionaires as we know by now are rule-breakers, but his decision caused friction at the time.

Much of the thinking at Aspen is not dissimilar to that at Investec. Both Saad and Koseff told me that they rewarded risk-takers and did not punish failure, provided the failure was the result of a genuine and sensible effort to grow the business. Neither men tolerated repeat offenders, and certainly if the same person made the same mistake twice, he or she would be dismissed without question. Both men were always on the lookout for deals.

'If it's in our patch, and life is tough, then it can present an opportunity, but if it's in our patch and life is running, then everyone is chasing the same opportunity and prices are too high, we give it a miss,' Koseff said to me.

For Saad, if an investment banker presented his board with a transaction, they would routinely ignore the deal as it was probably overpriced and would likely have been offered elsewhere – this also raised the risk of time-consuming bidding wars. Rather, Aspen relied on its own networks to identify transactions and conclude them quickly before the broader market was aware of them. It was a strategy that stood them in good stead, but like so many rapid-expansion stories, they grew too fast and took on too much debt. The company is now adjusting and consolidating, having sold off an infant-formula business in China and another significant operation in Japan. The only global conglomerate to be headquartered in Umhlanga appears to have avoided the Icarus effect of crashing into the ocean after flying too close to the sun and has opted, sensibly, to control its own rate of descent to sustainability.

What started out as a producer of generic antiretroviral drugs for the South African market rapidly became the most geographically diverse business operating out of this country, and it acted quickly to take the opportunities as they presented themselves. Soon after becoming the biggest generics producer in Australia, Saad realised they'd managed as a South African company to disrupt all too easily the Australian market's biggest player, Mylan, so they moved their business from generics to speciality pharmaceuticals almost overnight. Like Gore's Discovery, a complex business is harder to replicate.

While it is unclear where the next Discovery, Shoprite or Anglo American will come from, what is certain is that without growth the next generation of business leaders are going to find it hard to build enterprises that will provide the jobs that the South African economy so desperately needs.

CHAPTER 8

· · · · · · · · · · · ·

The economy

'It's the economy, stupid.'
– Bill Clinton campaign strategist James Carville

If we can't get growth moving, then everything else we aspire to comes to nothing. The great political cartoonist Zapiro captured the disparities in South Africa's economy best in a classic sketch in February 2000. A small boy is seated outside a tin shack while his mother, with a baby strapped to her back in a blanket, is washing clothes by hand in a puddle of water. Behind them in the distance is the gleaming skyline of Johannesburg – the symbol of a city built on the back of the gold first discovered on the Witwatersrand in 1884.

The little boy quips: 'You'll be glad to know that according to the analysts, the economic fundamentals are in place.'

His mother is unconvinced and scowls at the fact that her lived experience is nothing like the averages that analysts' reports parrot as evidence of an improving South Africa.

South Africa is the 24th-largest country in the world by area. It is the second-largest but most developed economy within Africa.

There are occasions when it is bigger than Nigeria, but that is dependent on which Nigerian exchange rate you use to convert their GDP into dollars. Many global organisations, such as the G20, like to have representation from all regions, and as a result South Africa is typically included as the member representing sub-Saharan Africa, giving the country a higher profile and voice than it might otherwise attract. South Africa represents about 0.4% of global GDP, and while it plays a far bigger political role in the world than the size of its economy suggests, through its work on the UN Security Council, in BRICS and other global bodies, its status is slipping and its prospects are dimming.

In an $86tn world, South Africa's annual GDP comes to $0.37tn, or just 0.43% of the total. That's about the same as Israel, though they have a seventh of our population.

Within South Africa, political parties can make all the big promises they like: land reform, distribution of wealth, National Health Insurance, better education, reliable electricity, and a clean and safe water supply. None of it can happen without money. And there will not be enough money without growth.

Unemployment is rising annually as the economy drags itself along on bloodied knuckles at rates below population growth. Consequently, hundreds of thousands of people every year become a statistic and join those looking for jobs. The situation can't go on like this, and the government knows it. 'South Africa's current economic trajectory is unsustainable; economic growth has stagnated, unemployment is rising and inequality remains high,' reads the introduction to a parcel of proposed economic reforms devised by National Treasury and posted online at the same time as they were emailed to cabinet in the second half of 2019. Everyone had access to the same information at the same time. It was a political masterstroke as it ensured that the document could not be undermined before it was publicly available. It could also not be watered down in cabinet or by government departments. Finance minister Tito Mboweni, usually a stickler for protocol, rules and processes, was breaking ranks. It was the clearest signal yet that the time for prevaricating over the issues afflicting the economy was past. The ratings downgrade clock was ticking ever louder and officials at the Treasury knew it was make or break for the country's hard-won credit rating.

Neither Mboweni nor President Cyril Ramaphosa, life-long ANC members, wants to be at the bridge when the economy goes down. Hence they are desperately trying to drag the cabinet into confronting the brutal realities besetting the country. Unless they can do so in a hurry and make policy reforms on their own terms, they will eventually have those forced upon them by lenders of last resort like the International Monetary Fund. It would be madness to allow this to happen as the ANC would then lose control of the economy.

Intellidex analyst Peter Attard Montalto described the policy document as 'incendiary, but marvellously evidence-based'. Rather than the vagueness of superficial 14-point and other shoot-from-the-hip plans proposed previously, the document set out particular interventions. It laid out plans to encourage growth, prioritising sectors for labour-intensive growth in areas such as tourism and agriculture, while lowering the crippling costs of doing business. It set out time frames over two-, five- and seven-year periods as a way of establishing building blocks for a new economy. But time, like money, is rapidly running out.

There are all kinds of economic arguments against a focus on GDP as a catch-all measure of whether life is getting better or not. As with a golf scorecard, GDP has no remarks column. If you get a hole-in-one after you shanked your shot into a passing golf cart, rolled through a shallow bunker before knocking your playing partner's ball at the lip of the cup before dropping in the hole, no one examining that card will ever know. That is the problem with GDP. The mindless pursuit of growth can have dire consequences. China is a case in point: the fastest-growing economy over three decades now has to deal with the serious environmental consequences of factory-led growth.

GDP as a measure has been around for three-quarters of a century after being developed by an economist called Simon Kuznets. We use it to rank countries in terms of performance. It's imperfect but it does one thing very well: it measures activity. If South Africa was a hospital patient, and GDP the measure of its pulse, the doctor would be telling relatives to get ready for the worst.

GDP makes no distinction between things that are positive for humanity and things that are negative. It measures everything equally as a growth contributor. A World Economic Forum paper on the subject explains it best: 'Kim Jong-un's warheads do just as well for GDP as hospital beds and apple pie.'

For South Africa right now, though, academic arguments are not particularly helpful. Without tax revenues, the ANC's vision of a state-centred developmental state, in which more than 17 million social grants of some form are paid monthly, cannot hope to function. A cynic might argue that the ANC's greatest asset is its ability to keep its citizens dependent on it. That dependence keeps voters coming back and renewing their commitment to the party every five years at the ballot box. However, the ANC's recent electoral performance has shown that voters are increasingly fearful of what will happen when the money does run out, and if nothing else, that should prompt a response. There is nothing like self-preservation to focus the mind.

You only have to analyse the Treasury's Budget Review documents from recent years to see the rapidly deteriorating picture of the country's finances. Mostly it's because there are not enough taxpayers and too little has been done to stop the looting of the fiscus.

As the budget deficit expands to beyond 6% of GDP and with the economy collapsing under the weight of Stage 6 load-shedding after having shown growth potential of just 0.3%–0.5% for the year in 2019, its slowest rate since 2016 and below the annual population growth of around 1.5%, the country is running out of choices as to how to tackle its multiple problems.

Governments become addicted to the power they wield, and it's only voters who are able to get rid of them. But in a populist world you do have to be careful what you wish for. You can rid yourself of the crowd that caused the problem and end up with an even more destructive force in power, as so many countries have learned to their cost over the past hundred years. Somehow, as an act of self-preservation Ramaphosa's government must either conjure up hundreds of billions of rand to keep funding failing state-owned enterprises or summon the courage to do the unthinkable and ask the private sector for help. Like any addict, it first has to admit it has a problem before any outside intervention will have the desired result.

Eskom is by far the biggest culprit in the basket of failures, after more than a decade of mismanagement, grotesque incompetence, corruption and delinquency. As serious politically for the ANC but not as catastrophic as the R454bn debt burden at the power utility are the SABC, Denel and SAA. All to a greater or lesser extent form part of the hundreds of thousands of column inches written on state capture.

In late October 2019, after another round of unscheduled load-shedding the week before, the president described, in a newly instituted weekly newsletter, the sheer scale of Eskom's debt as 'daunting' and cautioned that further bailouts would put even more pressure on a constrained fiscus – this was code for 'If we don't get this sorted out quickly, we are in serious trouble.' Those chickens came home to roost again in December 2019 as the lights went out, ironically on 9/12, the fourth anniversary of the unceremonious sacking of finance minister Nhlanhla Nene by President Zuma.

Treasury proposals to slash R300bn in spending over the next three years are ambitious and probably a case of too little, too late. Nor are they politically palatable, but unless Cyril Ramaphosa and his finance minister can convince their colleagues of the importance of the cutbacks, the whole country is in trouble.

Stanlib economist Kevin Lings has created a matrix of 12 economic indicators that he has been measuring now for two years, and his accumulated data has shown that there has been no marked improvement in key economic outcomes since Cyril Ramaphosa ascended to power. So much for the New Dawn that was so rapturously welcomed. He concedes that much other work has been done to stabilise the country on the edge of collapse, and those building blocks need to be in place before any serious reform agenda can take hold. But progress is slow and the chances of a recovery are crippled as a result. The electricity shortage and the appeal to miners to cease operations until the grid was stable enough to continue showed the severity of the situation.

The reality is that the burden of keeping the country afloat has fallen squarely onto the shoulders of the privileged, which, in South Africa's case, form a tiny tax base. They too are disgruntled about the burden placed upon them, and this has led to a spike in emigration. Government needs to find a way to show appreciation to taxpayers or risk losing even more to the growing wave of emigrants.

I sat next to a billionaire at an event recently (because that's how I roll – and I can now confirm that business prowess does not transfer via osmosis) who was bemused and frustrated by the regular tax audits to which he is subjected. 'Every year they demand supporting documents and evidence of income and expenditure, and it's complicated and can take my accountants weeks to compile what they want. We send it, and then get the all-clear. It's frustrating. They have been doing it to me for years and wasting their time. I take compliance seriously. They should know by now that I am a good taxpayer, and should use that time and energy to find people not paying their tax,' he said. It's a widely echoed sentiment.

Worries about wealth taxes, the likely introduction of a new tax regime for those working outside the country, rising costs on capital gains, transfer duties and concerns about prescribed assets being applied to retirement funds, are all causing many who can afford to move, to look for new homes in jurisdictions which they believe to be less demanding on their pockets.

According to Stats SA, the country has about 33 million adults aged between 20 and 65. Of those, just 7.6 million, or 23% of the adult population, contribute directly to income taxes. It's even more stark when you consider that South Africa's overall population is somewhere between 57 and 60 million. At best, fewer than 12% of people living in South Africa pay any form of income tax. Just over 5%, or 3.3 million people, pay 90% of the country's income taxes.

Just 121,000 of the country's taxpayers earn more than R1.5m a year and pay taxes at the marginal rate of 45%. They earn 14% of the country's taxable income, yet pay 29% of all the personal taxes. It's the way South Africa's progressive tax system is structured. The more you earn, the more you pay. It's accepted as a fact of life. What that segment resents is the looting of that money. They are also the most globally mobile part of the population and thus pose the biggest risk to the fiscus should they depart. More than a tenth of the country's entire revenue is dependent on just 0.2% of the population.

'If just 12,000 individuals were to decide to leave (10% of top earners), you would lose R16bn in taxes,' warns Bernard Sacks, a tax partner at Mazars. 'This is where we are very vulnerable.'

Economist Mike Schussler notes that R16bn is equivalent to the amount that the National Treasury raises from 2.4 million tax-payers earning less than R150,000 a year. As much as the country's shrinking trade union movement may resent their existence and as much as they are the whipping boys of the Gucci-wearing faux left, the small, increasingly endangered pool of wealthy South Africans remains a valuable source of income.

Sacks adds that high-income earners are also an economy's biggest spenders, and their departure would negatively impact on consumption taxes like VAT as well as fuel and other lesser taxes. Many are likely to be employers, and if they move their businesses abroad, it would lead to domestic job losses.

Personal income taxes make up the single biggest contribution to the fiscus. With such heavy dependence on the goodwill of just over 3 million people to keep paying their taxes, the country is particularly vulnerable, especially in view of mounting evidence that the tax base is gradually being eroded. A growing number of the country's most highly skilled white-collar workers and professionals are emigrating, frustrated by the high levels of public-sector corruption and incompetence, collapsing public services, and a decline in personal safety levels. While some either dodge paying the fiscus what is due or pay experts to advise on aggressive tax structuring, many others are simply emigrating. Government either cannot or will not provide emigration statistics. SARS commissioner Edward Kieswetter admits he is concerned about the shrinking tax base.

The more people in work and earning a decent salary, the higher the country's tax revenues. However, record unemployment and anecdotal evidence gleaned from falling demand for private schooling, reportedly the result of emigration, by listed private-education firms such as ADvTECH and Curro, show that the country's tax base is being eroded.

The second-biggest chunk of money that flows into the fiscus is contributed by everyone, in the form of domestic taxes on goods and services, in proportion to what they spend and where they choose to spend it. Because of their sophisticated collection mechanisms, they are harder to avoid than personal taxes. About 34% of the nation's tax revenue comes from consumption taxes, most of it, about 25% of the total taxes collected, from the raised 15% VAT rate, which in a slowing economy did not actually raise the increased amounts budgeted for. Following the first, deeply unpopular hike in VAT since its implementation nearly 30 years ago, retailers reported a drop in sales as cash-strapped households cut back on spending.

For all the fanfare around 'sin taxes', they make only a small contribution to overall revenue. Beer sales alone raise 1% of all taxes in South Africa, a little more than taxes on tobacco products. Less than 3% comes from excise duties on products like alcohol and tobacco, whereas the ever-increasing taxes on fuel, which everyone pays either through filling up their own vehicles or using public transport, come to about 6% of all taxes collected.

Amid uncertainty around land reform, and as a consequence of the higher rates of tax on more expensive properties, the amount collected in transfer duties declined in 2018 for the first time, from R8.2bn to R7.72bn, or just 0.63% of the total taxes collected.

All of this, of course, excludes the taxes levied on citizens at local level. Rates and taxes in most urban areas have been rising above inflation in an effort to redress a lack of spending over decades in poorer areas.

For long-suffering taxpayers, there is a breaking point that can be reached in their tolerance of their tax burdens. If the e-tolls rebellion is anything to go by, they are fed up with high levels of wasteful expenditure and more concerned than ever about the level of corruption in government, which President Ramaphosa told delegates at the October 2019 Financial Times Summit on Africa had cost anything from R500bn to R1tn during the Zuma years. SARS is apparently concerned about compliance levels since the hijacking of the revenue service under former commissioner Tom Moyane. The reality is that South African tax rates cannot be raised much further.

While a handful of taxpayers have been keeping South Africa afloat, that is no longer enough. Given that the national debt has ballooned to unsustainable levels, that there is little growth to speak of, and that the regulatory environment is hardly encouraging to small-business innovation and start-ups, the tax base will shrink further unless there is urgent remedial action.

While the National Treasury has consistently budgeted for increases in revenue, SARS has failed to collect the money that government had expected it would. Government budgeted R1.422tn for collection in February 2019, but it was clear at the midpoint of the tax year that the target would be missed. A combination of job losses, lower-than-expected wage increases, and under-pressure corporate profits all contributed to the shortfall.

Growth is pivotal for the country. And it can't just be consumption-led, which can happen if you slash lending rates to boost short-term confidence. Tax cuts can have the same effect, as has been seen in Donald Trump's America. This sleight of hand provides only the illusion of progress. There has to be jobs-rich, inclusive growth.

Ratings agencies and global lenders could not be clearer about the issues on which they are demanding reform if South Africa is going to be treated seriously in other parts of the world. The country needs reforms that provide policy certainty, increased competition across the economy including state-owned enterprises, an improved quality of education, improved health care, and the stabilisation of Eskom to ensure a steady, affordable supply of unbroken energy. South Africa needs to ensure that spectrum is freed up and that tourists (and citizens) are safe. It must offer incentives for job creators and exporters, encourage local manufacture, and, probably most important of all, provide all South Africans with a stake in the long-term future. For those at present without, South Africans need to be given a title deed to a piece of land, which cannot be traded for a period of time, and whose security of tenure requires the payment of modest rates and taxes and of basic services like electricity and waste removal. Mostly, South Africans need to know the lights will stay switched on as long as they pay for the power.

Much of this can be achieved by co-opting a private sector eager to secure its own long-term future by creating a sustainable economy. But the state cannot be effective without a highly skilled and competent bureaucracy. There are already projects under way where corporates second talented staff to government departments to assist with improving administrative processes. It's a delicate subject. Government cannot be seen to require external help and the companies doing the work don't want to be seen rubbing civil service faces in their own failings.

No matter where you look, there is mounting evidence of governance failures. Whether it's the grotesque levels of unemployment, education failings, housing shortages, political uncertainty or the risk of economic downgrades, the country dances on the very edge of self-destruction, occasionally peering over into the abyss of failure and social collapse.

As delegates gathered at the World Economic Forum on Africa 2019 in early September of that year, bands of predominantly local men took to burning and looting shops owned by foreigners in several parts of South Africa. Incidents of xenophobia have been happening with alarming frequency over recent years, and the latest explosion of rage spread quickly across poorer parts of South Africa, sparking an angry reaction at home and overseas and retaliatory attacks on South African-owned businesses elsewhere on the continent.

At the same time, protests erupted outside the Cape Town International Convention Centre, fuelled by mounting anger at the country's rising incidents of femicide. The rape and murder of UCT student Uyinene Mrwetyana caused simmering concerns to reach boiling point at the same time as the latest round of xenophobic attacks. The issues seem unrelated, but there is an underlying theme. Most perpetrators are angry, predominantly young, hopeless South African men. It's that growing sense of

hopelessness about the future that is leading to mounting anger in communities, says Tracey Chambers, co-founder of The
Clothing Bank, an NGO that takes clothing, previously destined
for landfill and incineration, and distributes it to more than 3,000
women whom it has trained to run micro-enterprises. They select
items from centralised distribution centres to which retailers deliver end-of-season unsold lines. The Clothing Bank then passes
on those clothes at vastly discounted prices, and the women on
the programme take them to sell at open-air markets.

The clothing is typically brand-new, often without any de-
fects, and is bought and sold in a manner that previously did
not exist. Chambers, who had worked in the finance division at
Woolworths where she spotted the line item for clothes marked
for destruction, convinced CEO Ian Moir that her organisation
would not be undermining the Woolies brand if it took unsold
lines and put them into a market that the company was not reaching anyway. So successful was the pilot scheme that other South
African retailers came on board.

'These women are able to feed, educate and clothe their children,'
says Chambers. 'But it's presented another problem. They are going home to partners who in many cases cannot find opportunities
for themselves, and it can lead to deep resentment and, in some
cases, violence in the home.' So she approached Clicks and discovered that they too were disposing of faulty electrical equipment
that customers had brought back to be exchanged and, because of
mass-production techniques, was not worth their while to repair.
Instead, Chambers is taking in the faulty electrical equipment and
training men to repair and retail the products themselves in much

the same way as women have done with clothing. It's yielding positive results. But the overall unemployment crisis in the country is a time bomb, which, if not effectively addressed, can scupper any hope of a sustainable, prosperous future for South Africa.

South Africa is not unique in its growing aversion to the excesses of the super-rich. French economist Thomas Piketty has seen his global notoriety grow since he published *Capital in the 21st Century* in 2013 in which he strongly argued for wealth taxes on multi-generational wealth. It's become a popular theme, too, in the US for Democratic Party nominees vying to stand against Donald Trump in the 2020 elections.

Piketty's central thesis points to a situation which exists in South Africa today: when the rate of return on capital is greater than the rate of economic growth over long periods of time, wealth becomes concentrated in the hands of a few. It is that concentration of wealth and unequal distribution which ultimately lead to social instability, as is evident not just in Chile and Lebanon but increasingly also in South Africa. Sasria, the state-owned insurer which provides cover against civil disobedience, says it has seen a hundredfold increase in the number of claims since 2007 and the cost of claims rise from R14m to R1.4bn over the period amid a rising tide of public anger at the lack of service delivery and other local-government failings.

Piketty contributes to the populist playbook by arguing that there should be a system of progressive wealth taxes globally to help reduce inequality. In South Africa, the well-intentioned disclosure of directors' pay, which was designed to provide transparency and even a cap on some of its worst excesses, has simply put the vast inequalities of the South African workplace in the public domain. In a country where the lowest-paid worker would need to perform their task for 90 minutes to pay for the CEO's first cappuccino of the day, it's hardly surprising that even people with jobs are frustrated – never mind the 5 million with little prospect of even getting a minimum wage.

It all comes down, it would seem, to happiness. Happiness is a fluid concept. There are poor agrarian societies where people live in relative poverty that might be described as 'happy' whereas people earning many times more and commuting for hours daily from home to their place of work are often miserable. Research by Gallup published in 2018, after being conducted over a three-year period, found world happiness has declined, particularly as a result of a sustained downward trend in India. In terms of emotions, such as worry, sadness and anger, there have been marked increases in Asia and Africa. The *World Happiness Report* may sound flaky but the trends found in 2019 are interesting in that the report ranks 156 countries according to how happy their citizens perceive themselves to be. South Africa came in at 106th – just behind Benin, Congo-Brazzaville, Gabon and Laos, and only two positions ahead of Venezuela. People in Libya, Lebanon and Nigeria reported higher levels of happiness than in South Africa.

The report contains a chapter penned by Professor Jeffrey Sachs, who is director of the UN Sustainable Development Solutions Network. He focuses on the epidemic of addictions and unhappiness in America, a rich country yet one where happiness has been declining rather than rising. Those addictions come in many forms, from substance abuse and gambling to a fixation with social media. Serious institutions like the London School of Economics take note of the research and suggest it should give governments a wake-up call.

Among the implications of levels of happiness is the propensity to vote for governing parties. It goes some way to explaining the explosion of populism worldwide and the growth in authoritarian states which claim to offer better alternatives than the incumbents. The warning to the South African government from studies like this is that facts seldom matter in an argument when it comes to personal or group happiness. The facts, it would seem, seldom have a positive impact on overall levels of happiness.

South Africa has, despite the negativity around corruption, inequality and the rising perception of injustice in society, taken serious strides in improving the lives of more of its citizens than previously. According to the Institute of Race Relations (IRR), social-housing delivery has had a positive impact on South African society, even though there is a very strong sense that the situation with informal housing represents a growing crisis. The reality, contrary to the claims of populists, is that on average the lives of most South Africans have improved since 1994. Averages are, however, a mathematical construct. It's like telling someone with their feet in the fire and their head in the fridge that on average they should be perfectly comfortable.

Nelson Mandela's government inherited a state not only politically and morally bankrupt, but financially too. Debt to GDP was then running at 48%. The new administration succeeded in cutting that figure to 27% as it introduced financial discipline in a recovering economy. The interest savings thus created funded that initial safety net and served to alleviate extreme poverty.

According to the IRR, ten formal houses have been built for every shack in South Africa over the past quarter of a century. Back in 1994, 7 million families had access to clean water. That number has now more than doubled to 15 million. There are 7 million cars in private ownership today compared to 3 million back then, and while it is harder to measure education outcomes, in 1985 there were 200,000 (mostly white) students in tertiary education; the number has now grown to about a million.

New HIV infections are down by 50%, and average life expectancy has shot up from a paltry 54 in 2002 to about 64, thanks to the introduction of antiretrovirals. The child-mortality rate has nearly halved to 43/100,000, and despite the fear that public health is going to hell in a handbasket, the number of GPs in public service has doubled to 14,000, while the number of nurses has grown by 62%. Violent crime has declined markedly since 1994. There are half the murders that there were in 1994.

Of course problems abound – many of them. Growth in 2019 failed to meet the 3% target anticipated at the start and instead the year very nearly delivered a second recession in a decade primarily due to the meltdown in electricity supply in the first and fourth quarters of the year. South Africa's failure to deal with its electricity crisis over more than a decade is symptomatic of a far bigger problem. The inability to identify problems timeously, strategise on how best to resolve them quickly and efficiently using the very best resources and skills at our disposal, and then deliver on those plans is probably the country's greatest weakness. If acknowledged, it could become the catalyst for recovery.

CHAPTER 9

· · · · · · · · · · · · ·

Jobs

'In South Africa, pressure is not having a job.'
– Rassie Erasmus

About five or six years ago I met an executive director at the insurance company Momentum. Frank Magwegwe had an unusual story. After being fired from his job in an Eastern Cape hotel for helping himself to the drinks, he boarded a train for Johannesburg where he had a relative. His ticket got him only as far as Bloemfontein, where he slept rough for a couple weeks while working in a fish and chips shop to earn his ticket to complete his journey.

Once in Johannesburg, he managed to stay with his relative for just three weeks before being thrown out. In the winter of 1993 he slept rough where he could while looking for any opportunity that might present itself. It was bitterly cold and he was routinely chucked out of some of the best sleeping spots by police, who in those days patrolled Joubert Park and other parts of town, moving on rough sleepers.

Frank befriended a hawker called Evelyn, who had her own

stall, and he would help her out in return for left-over fruit and vegetables that she'd been unable to sell during the day. He was useful to have around. He was strong, enthusiastic and had a head for numbers. It wasn't long before his benefactor was also giving him a little bit of cash. He saved the money and kept sleeping rough while setting up a stall of his own.

At first, he operated just one stall, then two and then a third, eventually employing people to run them for him. He would get up in the dark, make his way to the Johannesburg fresh-produce market to procure his wares for the day, deliver them to his team and then head off to the Johannesburg Public Library where he would read voraciously and learn everything he could before heading back to stock-take and collect the money his stalls had earned during the day.

After several weeks at the library, he was approached by a Mrs Zimmerman, who had observed his visiting patterns and reading habits and asked what he was up to. Initially concerned that he was about to have his library privileges revoked, he was pleased to learn she simply wanted to help an enthusiastic young man making his way in the world.

She advised him on how to apply for a bursary to Wits, where he eventually obtained a BSc in Statistics and Actuarial Science. Later he gained his Master's degree from the University of Pretoria. After years in the corporate world, Magwegwe now coaches others through Thrive, his own financial-wellness consultancy.

Magwegwe's story is one of grit, determination and ultimate triumph over extreme adversity. To be able to wake up every morning after snatching sleep in far-from-ideal conditions, get cleaned up and presentable on a daily basis for months on end, and not only survive but thrive is extraordinary. Fortunately, that spirit of grit and determination is not as rare as you might think it is.

In my day job I am extraordinarily privileged to run a two-hour business radio show. I go to work every day not quite knowing what to expect. There is always going to be some salacious gossip, or the odd shock-horror story about a company struggling through tough times, and markets will go up some days and down the next.

Few days could beat the one on which I received this letter:

Hi Bruce

I wanted to share with you how you helped me transition into business. I tried to capture everything in this timeline.

In 2009, I was homeless and partly lived in a park in Westdene called Kingston Frost Park. My prized possession was a phone which had an FM radio. I charged it daily to listen to 702. I liked all the shows, but your show was the most fascinating. I called it my business school. I sold cigarettes and mints, and I tried to apply your principles.

Between 2009 and 2011 I did several odd jobs as a casual worker: security guarding, truck loading and carpentry. I kept listening to your show throughout.

In 2011 I was encouraged to start a proper business. I started an informal handyman company focusing on general repair work. In April of that year, there was a protracted Pikitup strike. I hired a bakkie, and I sent you an email offering to be a solution for desperate households. You tweeted the email, and a flood of calls came through. Between

2011 and 2013 I collected rubbish from different households, but after the strike, the listeners became a pipeline for my handyman business.

In 2013 a listener heard about the Awethu Project on the radio, probably on your show, and shared the information. I joined the incubator, and the rest is history. Today, I am the Chief Executive of a development consultancy called Driven. We focus on inclusive development, mainly economic and financial inclusion, and lately also disability inclusion with special-needs children in peri-urban townships. We are a 10-man team with an office in Rosebank. On 12 April 2019, we will celebrate five years as an entity. It will be eight years since I sent you the email. And 10 years of listening to your show.

I have moved from selling cigarettes for 90c each to discussing financial-inclusion interventions for entire communities with budgets that run into millions.

Warm regards
Owen Muzambi, CEO – Driven

The country needs 100,000 Owens. If his story doesn't move you, you have a heart made of granite. The reality is that millions of people are trapped in situations like those of Frank and Owen. Few manage to break out. South Africa's official jobs statistics make for devastating reading.

Unemployment has been so high for so long that for those in work it's taken for granted. For those cast out or unable to break into the increasingly exclusive club of 'the employed', it's a soul-destroying reality. Future generations are likely to regard our failure to tackle this issue as a human-rights abuse.

The latest statistics show that there are 10.3 million people out of work. That's considerably more than the number who pay income tax. It's not a sustainable ratio.

So much of our sense of self is defined by what we do for a living. It was a fact not lost on 2019 World Cup-winning coach Rassie Erasmus, who despite the euphoria of managing the best rugby team in the world at that moment responded to a question about the pressure of the tournament in this way: 'In South Africa, pressure is not having a job. Pressure is having one of your close relatives murdered. There are a lot of problems in South Africa – which are real pressure. Rugby shouldn't be something that creates pressure; rugby should be something that creates hope.'

There is no greater reality check than bumping into an old acquaintance and asking how they are and what they are up to, only to be met with: 'I can't find a job.' I defy you to consider what you would do next beyond the platitudes of 'I'll see what I can find. Oh, is that the time?' before you scuttle off. Unemployment is a crisis that few of us know how to confront. But there are some smart solutions which can help to alleviate some of the issues.

Ultimately, the only tonic for mass unemployment is growth.

What's the difference between a recession and a depression? It's an old and tasteless joke but seems appropriate right now. A recession is when your neighbour loses his job. A depression is when you lose yours.

South Africa has structurally high unemployment. One of the main reasons is that we are a consumption-based economy. If you consider that the composition of the JSE is made up mostly of services companies rather than manufacturing businesses, you will quickly grasp the problem. Our industrial base has been denuded over time. A lack of competitiveness, driven by a lack of skills and innovation, has made South Africa, with some notable exceptions, an industrial backwater. We import most of what we consume, which means we are exporting our money in return for products that we probably should produce more of here.

Population growth has outstripped economic growth for the past five years, and as a result the economy cannot absorb the number of people of working age. This is at the heart of the problem.

Youth unemployment, defined as affecting people between 15 and 34, nudged 55% in 2019, as official figures showed that a record number of adults could not find work. The official unemployment rate sits at more than 29%, and if you include those so disheartened by their failure to find a job opportunity that they have given up looking for one, the total number of people out of work expands to around 37%.

Countries with far lower rates of unemployment face far higher levels of civil strife than we see daily. Governments have fallen for less. Something else is thus at play in South Africa, and this has largely to do with our two-speed economy. Many people in this country find opportunities in the informal sector. They are often poorly paid in cash and, because they are in survival mode, don't declare their income so that they can also access social grants. They are thus impossible to track. Only a few, like Frank Magwegwe, ever break out.

The sociologist GG Alcock points out in his books *KasiNomics* and *KasiNomic Revolution* that many people in poorer communities rely on their instincts in creating survivalist businesses, which are unregistered and untraceable by statisticians and tax authorities. Although this strategy alleviates some of the pain of abject poverty, the need for real formal-sector jobs remains.

'*Ngiyasebenza angi namusebenzi*' is a common reply Alcock gets when enquiring about people's employment status in townships. 'I don't have a job, but I work.' Alcock has found that many people who hustle for a living, trying their hand at everything from breeding chickens for slaughter in someone else's backyard, to renting out a room in their own yard to informal street traders, would happily throw this up in an instant for a job. And it's usually a government job. These have high value because if you can get into government employment, the world is your oyster. The problem is that even the government is considering the future of its hiring policies and some departments, because of budgetary constraints, are not replacing many of those who leave.

For Alcock, *KasiNomics* is about revealing the considerable opportunities that exist in the informal sector. He talks about BMW-driving providers of *kota*, wholesome township street food, and of women who put their children through school by renting out patches of land for backyard dwellers, of informal car washes and hair salons where the painstaking craft of braiding is practised for hours on end. Billions of rands' worth of business is executed in the cash economy of townships, little of which gets quantified, and the people who work in the informal jobs are never counted as working.

Alcock also consults to large corporates seeking to access the

Kasi economy. Despite in many cases decades of operating in South Africa's formal, high-speed economy, they have no idea of how to begin. 'There's this massive world of entrepreneurs and micro-businesses in this informal sector that needs to be recognised, and in some ways there's an opportunity for businesses to partner with them and network with them. On the other hand, it's an opportunity for township people to actually recognise the opportunities around them, as opposed to looking outside of the township,' Alcock says.

One couple retails 3,000 helpings of *vetkoek* every single morning for R1 each, as well as hundreds of rand of coffee and tea, and can earn as much as R3,500 a day, tax-free. And they are not VAT-registered either. They are running margins of 40%–50% and can earn R30,000 a month working from 3 am to 10 am daily. Another woman sells food items at a school and has occupied the same position for 26 years. She works for less than four hours a day and takes home about R6,000 a month. Alcock is particularly proud of the fact that he managed to convince enough *kota* sellers to introduce slices of processed cheese into their offering, so that Parmalat now sells R1.5bn worth of product into a market that it previously believed it could not reach.

For far too many South Africans, their daily reality is unemployment. The longer this remains so, the less confidence they have in their own ability to provide for themselves and their families. This leads to a growing sense of hopelessness and despair. The rising tide of unemployment is South Africa's biggest challenge. It destroys hope. If you cannot imagine a South Africa in which you and your family are better off in five years than they are now, you have nothing to lose.

Almost four in every ten people in the labour force do not have a formal job, and the longer they stay out of work, the less likely they are to ever find employment. All this poses a massive challenge for political and social stability. It is going to take a significant shift in official policy to encourage the creation of small businesses that will produce the jobs which the economy needs in order to become sustainable.

Tashmia Ismail is the CEO of the Youth Employment Service (YES), a government-backed, private-sector initiative designed to provide young people with work experience. President Cyril Ramaphosa, himself forced to lay off workers on one of his farms near Badplaas in Mpumalanga owing to the parlous state of the economy, boldly proclaimed that this initiative would yield a million jobs in three years. It's done nowhere near that number, but it has made steady inroads, acquiring an understanding of the dynamics of the labour market and helping more than 30,000 people as a result to find their way into internships funded mostly by large companies.

We can scoff at government's attempts at intervening in the jobs market and its talk of 'creating jobs'. It's been very effective at creating jobs in the civil service, to the extreme detriment of the country as so much money is spent on wages for civil servants that there is too little left to perform the work that actually benefits the poor. You can throw up your hands in disgust and add to the drone of discontent, or you can think about the problem differently. Where there is crisis, there is opportunity.

At present there is a small technology revolution happening

in South Africa. One promising venture in the private sector involves teaching young people how to communicate with technology in the language it understands. The best part of this is that you don't need a university degree or even a matric, but simply the right aptitude and attitude to learning. If one considers World Bank statistics that half the world's 'employed' are self-employed, what better tool could you give young people than the skills to navigate the economy of the future? Now a lot of nonsense is spoken about the fourth industrial revolution and how it will somehow miraculously rescue the world from poverty and despair. What it does need, though, is skilled people to drive it.

Arlene Mulder is one of a growing army of technology warriors training young people to code. At WeThinkCode in Cape Town's Waterfront, anyone – mostly anyone between the ages of 16 and 34 – who passes an aptitude test can participate for nothing in a two-year coding programme that can see 18-year-old 'graduates' enter the job market with a R25,000-a-month salary. Demand is high, and slackers are not tolerated.

All companies increasingly need coding skills. What has been happening is that South African firms have been outsourcing many of the jobs they need doing to low-cost producers in places like India which are way ahead in terms of technology training. But, says Mulder, there is a growing trend towards building local skills. WeThinkCode is funded by the banking sector as a means to grow domestic skills.

'You have to think of coding as this superpower that allows you to create almost anything you can imagine, and so if you think about it in the South African context it's extremely important to solve problems,' says Mulder. 'In Silicon Valley they are worrying about problems like how to get hot coffee across town faster. In South Africa we have real problems that can be addressed with coding; name any problem, and coding can help you fix it, whether it be from water supplies to electricity, you name it.'

Aisha Pandor is the great-granddaughter of ZK Matthews, one of the leading members of the ANC in his day and the man who conceived of the Freedom Charter. Her mother is South Africa's minister of international relations, Naledi Pandor. Aisha has a PhD in Human Genetics and graduated with a business degree on the same day as her doctorate was conferred upon her at UCT.

'I started asking myself in my early twenties about how my work as a geneticist would help the country. I thought of sitting by myself in a lab doing research that might help twenty or thirty thousand people and I realised it was not the best place for me to apply my energy and potential, so I figured that starting a business would enable me to have a bigger impact.'

Like so many start-ups, SweepSouth was triggered by the desire to solve a personal problem and was inspired by the magic of travel and exposure to the world's best ideas. Pandor's domestic worker was on leave and, after a particularly tough family visit, she and her husband Alen Ribic, having experienced the ride-sharing app Lyft in the US, wondered whether the same principle that applies to firms like Uber would work in other service industries.

They gave up their day jobs, moved themselves and their kids in with her parents, and set about creating an app that would connect domestic workers with job opportunities. More than 70% of the 15,000 or so women who have signed up for SweepSouth to date were previously unemployed. Most of the rest had spare time that they needed to fill in order to pay their bills. The app provided the women with a service that offered access to a market of employers who may have wanted to hire occasional help but lacked the knowledge or an easy enough way to engage with those willing to do their housework. SweepSouth has turned people who were previously unemployed into breadwinners.

The app has also democratised domestic work in a way that has never happened before. Notoriously underpaid domestic workers can often become trapped in abusive relationships where they are obliged to work extended hours for little or no additional remuneration. With SweepSouth women have a choice about where and when they work and for whom. As with the ride-hailing apps, both parties in the transaction are able to check each other out beforehand.

The biggest difference here is that domestic work involves a relationship. You don't have a relationship with your Uber driver, apart from the five to twenty minutes during which you are in the car, and you don't mind who the next Uber driver is who comes to pick you up. The domestic work relationship is different, more intimate. The person you hire comes into your personal space and needs to quickly assess your personal preferences in your home. They also need to know that they are going to be safe, treated equitably and, what is important, paid for their efforts. There is a mutual rating mechanism that ensures a level of mutual accountability, which is not something that has traditionally been a feature of South Africa's domestic-work industry.

When Pandor and Ribic started out, smartphones were less

common than they are today. They had to put up surety to buy smartphones for every domestic worker who joined the platform. Their prediction that the devices would become cheaper and more common over time has held true, so there is less pressure now to supply devices as most women have their own.

The bulk of the marketing for SweepSouth was done by word of mouth. It spread from the helper to her neighbourhood, to taxi ranks and to townships. In a place where work is scarce, word of opportunities spreads quickly.

'I think people first and foremost need access to work, they need free access to work, and if they have skills they can provide, they have the right to earn in return for providing those skills,' Pandor says. 'We have one sweep star who, because of the flexibility that the platform gave her, was able to work and complete a law degree at the same time.'

SweepSouth now employs about 50 people directly, three of them former 'sweep stars' who have secured office jobs after showing their mettle on the platform, in addition to connecting 15,000 people with work on a regular basis.

The platform has had other spin-offs in that it has provided a new market for insurers, for example, who are coming on board as partners in the process and providing cost-effective income and life cover, at a rate that enables SweepSouth to make it available to the women on the platform at no cost to them.

'We've given thousands of people access to opportunities that they otherwise wouldn't have had. And so what we're trying to build and what my personal legacy is about is giving people access to dignified working opportunities,' says Pandor. Although some critics suggest that domestic work is demeaning, Pandor is quick to point out that a decent job is better than no job at all.

In 2019 SweepSouth raised nearly R50m in funding for an expansion into creating connections for tradespeople to help them reach new markets. How often have you driven past a hardware shop on a Saturday morning and seen people carrying signs reading 'Plumber', 'Tiler' or 'Gardener'? You have no way of knowing whether they are any good at their job, whether the pipes they install will leak, or whether the brickwork they lay will hold. Technology provides a mechanism for these guys to reach markets, and for those who want a job done to find someone to do it with a decent level of assurance that it will be done properly.

The R50m in funding came from a mix of backers. The biggest tranche came from a Naspers start-up fund called Foundry, which invested R30m, while the Michael and Susan Dell Foundation came up with another R13m. DJ Black Coffee, among other smaller investors, also put money into the venture. DJ Black Coffee (real name, Nkosinathi Innocent Maphumulo) is in demand to play gigs worldwide. He has five albums under his belt and is a successful entrepreneur in his own right. He is also investing in local start-ups, among them SweepSouth.

Another initiative in which he is involved is the wireless-payments system Yoco, founded by former cellphone industry colleagues Katlego Maphai, Carl Wazen, Bradley Wattrus and Lungisa Matshoba, who realised that big banks' expensive offerings were not ideal for small businesses. There are now 55,000 small companies on the platform. Maphai, who is CEO, sees great potential for additional products and services to be layered on top of the payments data which the devices create, with the potential for business-management systems and accounting software. 'The best part about a digital payment is that there is an immediate record that it happened, so if you can layer these additional services on top of that payment layer, then you are helping small businesses become more professional and grow,' says Maphai. Yoco has accumulated data that shows how revenues in small businesses increase when transactions are digitised. We have all been to a market and been tempted by a product costing a little more than the remaining cash in our wallet. The retailer can either get rid of his stock at a discount or run the risk of taking the item home at the end of the day. By being able to take card payments, sales increase.

Abalobi is an app designed in Cape Town to connect fishing communities with their customers, cutting out the middleman and providing traceability of the produce to the end consumer. It also provides business systems for fishermen. You may have been to a restaurant recently where you have been handed a wooden key ring in the shape of a fish with a QR code attached to it. Scan it and you will learn where and when the fish was caught, by whom, and more details about the community where the catch was made. In a world increasingly concerned about the sustainability of natural food resources, it's a win-win for users on both sides of the transaction.

All of these amazing innovations speak of the raw talent that is waiting to be recognised and supported in South Africa. As Aisha Pandor puts it: 'What a shame in South Africa ... that we have so many people who don't have access to work, and who can't make a living for themselves, and have to go cap in hand every month to get money from the government, and who don't have opportunities to uplift themselves. Above all, I think that is the most depressing thing about our country, and it will be the most depressing thing if people become hopeless, and they don't feel like they have opportunities.'

CHAPTER 10

The (not-so) mighty ZAR

'Soli Deo Gloria' – Motto on the R1 coin

There is a R1 coin propped up against my laptop as I write. It has a 3 cm diameter and is 3 mm thick. Embossed on it is a leaping springbok, which is jumping awkwardly over its written value: 1 Rand.

You have to squint to read 'Soli Deo Gloria'. That's Latin for 'Glory to God Alone'. (Even today's minuscule R1 coin retains the motto, which is odd for a secular state. Just as an aside, American banknotes still carry 'In God We Trust' on their reverse side. The statement first appeared on the Union 2c coins in 1864 during the American Civil War.)

Back home, flip over the chunky R1 coin, and the image of the man supposed to be Jan van Riebeeck, the first Dutch commander of the Cape, stares blankly back at you. It's imprinted with the words 'South Africa' and the date, 1966. Currencies are deeply political symbols that we carry with us all the time.

It's a great coin to hold. It feels like money should feel: it's weighty, it's big and fits neatly into the palm of an adult hand.

When you clench your fist over it, your hand doesn't quite close properly. It screams: 'Value'.

When you flick it into the air it makes a high-pitched pinging sound. Drop it on a tiled floor and it makes a satisfying racket.

It's still legal tender, but I don't recommend you use it. It's only going to buy you goods worth R1. Its actual value is much higher. I paid R200 at a coin dealer for mine. It has zero collectible value, as there are thousands like it in the market. But it does contain nearly an ounce of silver. That's what gives it its weight and makes it resonate when you flick it up in a game of 'heads or tails'.

If you had enough of them to make the economics work, and if it weren't illegal, you could melt them down and extract the silver, currently trading at $17/oz. This makes the silver content of the coin worth about R250. There would also be the cost of processing, and you would need lots of them to make the exercise worthwhile.

In my hands the coin serves a completely different purpose from that for which it was minted as a means of exchange. It's a great prop for telling stories about money. Audiences love to hold it and feel the weight of it in their hands. Invariably some will say they remember them. They probably remember the ones reissued in the mid-1970s, which were made of cheap alloy.

In between the two coin issues, the Reserve Bank printed a R1 note. It was muddy brown in colour. A different, more urbane image of Van Riebeeck stares out at you. The text is in English and Afrikaans, in which the government makes a pledge that if the note is presented at the Reserve Bank, the bearer will be paid 'Een Rand/One Rand', and it was signed by then governor TW de Jongh. Turn it over and you have an idyllic farming scene showing two massive woolly merino rams positioned among other agricultural produce and, bizarrely, a single-furrow plough that would have required a mule to pull it and a human to walk behind to direct the implement. South Africa was actually far more industrialised than that back then and farms were full of John Deere, Massey Ferguson and Ford tractors. It may have had something to do with Afrikaner nationalist iconography. The notes were widely used and became tatty and worn very quickly, hence the government decided to produce a new, similar-looking R1 coin made of cheaper materials in 1977. There was a blue R2 note, the purple R5 and the biggest denomination of the day, R10 – which was a lot of money back then.

Something happened in between the time my coin was minted and the mid-1970s when it was reissued in a fractionally smaller, thinner, much lighter alloy format. By then the value of money was no longer linked to the value of an underlying commodity.

Societies have used all kinds of coupons for millennia to represent value. The R200 note in your wallet is worth nothing other than the common expectation that you will be able to extract a product or service from another person who will be willing to give you an item of the same value for the amount of money you give him or her. They will then take that money and exchange it for something they want, and so on.

Coins have been around, as best we can tell, since about 600 BC. Archaeologists have found evidence of money being used then in what is modern-day Turkey. The Chinese were the first to issue paper money 1,200 years later. But there is evidence that people have used symbols of exchange for much longer. From rare shells to Egyptian metal rings to the iron crosses of Liberia, the dollar and bitcoin, a belief that our particular token of exchange has worth is all that lies between our being rich and having scraps of metal and paper stuffed into our wallets.

If you receive a payment into your bank account nowadays, there is no physical money changing hands. You accept that the company you work for has had a series of ones and zeros moved from its account to your account in a digital transaction that has increased your net worth and enabled you to open the app on your phone and make similar transfers to people who have trusted you to send them 'currency' in exchange for the things they have done for you or provided to you over the past month.

So, what exactly gives our modern forms of currency – whether it's an American dollar or a Japanese yen – value? Unlike early coins made of precious metals, most of what's minted today doesn't have much intrinsic value. However, it retains its worth for one of two reasons. It represents value. You believe a R1 coin will provide you with a product of equivalent value, which gives you the comfort to part with the coin in return for the product you buy.

Currencies used to be linked to the value of gold or, in the case of my coin, silver. Bronze and copper were also used. But as the war in Vietnam dragged on and America became increasingly indebted to fund the conflict, President Richard Nixon decided that the price of the US currency would rather be decided on financial markets. After centuries of money being backed by gold, fiat currencies were now backed by confidence. It gave governments the freedom to print as much or as little money as they wished. If they printed too much, prices went up as the value of the money in circulation declined.

There are few countries in the world that obsess about their currency in the same way as South Africans do. The currency occupies the tail end of every radio news bulletin. It makes its appearance on television as stern-faced business reporters discuss its movements with all of the intensity of a new parent discussing her baby's bowel habits. Its price adorns the front page of every news website, showing improvements in value in green or a worsening path in red.

The value of the rand is determined by supply and demand, just like any other commodity. If investors want to put money into South Africa, they might sell their dollars, euros or nairas and buy rands. If enough people invest, the rand gets stronger; if South African assets are being sold in large quantities, its value declines. The rand trades within a flexible exchange rate regime and its price fluctuates, sometimes violently, on a daily basis, often for reasons beyond South Africa's borders and beyond its control.

The demand for any currency relative to its supply determines its value in relation to other currencies. The rand will be stronger in a high-growth, low-inflation environment where there is strong demand for the country's goods and services. That's often the reason why, when our trading partners are doing well, we do well too, as their demand for what we produce rises. The big problem is that South Africa is not exporting nearly enough, and that's because manufacturing is down in the dumps.

One of the factors guarding the relative value of the rand at present is the high interest-rate differential between ourselves and many more developed countries. Whereas interest rates in many parts of the developed world have turned negative, which means it costs money to lend to governments like Germany for example, South Africa's higher rates attract capital. Despite the fact that inflation in South Africa is almost nonexistent compared to the past, the Reserve Bank has opted to keep rates high relative to where they could be if our economy was stronger. The prime lending rate decided at the last meeting of the Monetary Policy Committee in November 2019 stayed at 10%. That is a good yield if you have to pay your own central bank to deposit money with it. And even though 2019 showed strong selling of South African bonds ahead of a widely anticipated ratings downgrade by Moody's in 2020, the rand held its level relatively well.

A big negative factor impacting on our currency is the high current account deficit. We import more than we export, and as the deficit grows, it puts downward pressure on the currency as our demand for imports outstrips the demand for our exports, and we have to buy greater amounts of foreign exchange than other countries buy of our rand. South Africa therefore needs more foreign currency than is coming into the country and, as a result, demand for the rand drops and the currency weakens as we are forced to buy the currencies of other countries in order to pay them for their exports.

Confidence is a key factor for the currency. As many South Africans give up on the future value of the rand and export their local currency to environments where they believe their wealth will be better protected, there is further downward pressure on the currency. This contributes to a slow-burn self-fulfilling prophecy and to mounting social instability. Confidence matters. A country perceived to have fewer negative issues weighing down on its economic performance is likely to have a stronger currency than one that is constantly on the back foot.

The value of the rand does not just depend on real-world fundamentals, though. It is also a tradable commodity – about $50bn worth of rand is traded daily. You don't need to be engaged in buying currencies for the exchange of goods and services. You can also sit in your underwear in your bedroom trading currencies on your phone as a means to make money. Odds are you will be wiped out eventually by experienced currency traders whose volumes, algorithms and experience will see you carried out in a virtual body bag – it's not recommended for amateurs, no matter what the ads on Facebook tell you.

It seems crazy that a crisis in one part of the world can have an impact on another. South Africa experienced its first serious currency crash in 1997, sparked by a crisis in Argentina, which saw a sharp devaluation in the value of the rand. Turmoil in China after the country revalued its currency in 2015 saw the rand lose 26% of its value in the six months after the event. The fact that South Africa's politics were worsening at the time didn't help matters either – the sacking of Nhlanhla Nene as finance minister at the end of that year simply made matters worse. But the reason for the weakness was external rather than internal.

While South Africa tends to struggle from import-inflation

pressures during bouts of currency weakness, the fact that the rand has softened in value over time has meant that several of the country's industries have enjoyed inbuilt protections – notably mining, receives a benefit every time the currency weakens due to the fact that the commodities it produces are priced globally in dollars, while its costs are rand denominated. That means it is able to be more globally competitive against lower-cost producers from other parts of the world.

Tourism receipts also tend to pick up when the currency is weaker. As a long-haul destination that is expensive to reach, the country really has to fight for every foreign visitor in a highly competitive global tourism market. Recent years have been exceptions to the rule, owing to the fact that Cape Town, the country's biggest tourism drawcard, ran almost disastrously short of water. Another negative factor was the lunatic changes to the country's visa regime, which saw a reported 10,000 families turned away at foreign airports because they didn't have unabridged birth certificates included with their recognised travel documents. This bureaucratic madness has subsequently been checked, but much damage was done to a massive foreign exchange-earning industry.

South Africans' obsession with the value of the currency is understandable. If the level of a country's currency is a measure of your global wealth, or of testing the risk appetite of foreign investors, then it is a very useful tool.

The currency blowout of 9/12, for example, sent a very quick signal that financial markets were deeply concerned with the sudden changes to the leadership of the National Treasury. It provided the banking industry in particular with the leverage it needed to force President Jacob Zuma to change his mind and swap Des van Rooyen for Pravin Gordhan as finance minister. In the same way that the pound has lost value substantially against the dollar since Britain voted in a referendum to leave the European Union, the rand has provided an emergency release valve, indicating immediate, current concerns about the economic future of the country.

Currencies are nothing more than a mechanism for measuring the value of an exchange in a particular country. It's an expression of confidence in a country. Why is the US dollar so valuable and the Venezuelan bolivar not? Confidence; a belief that the currency will have buying power into the future. Take that away, and you end up with a crisis like the one which played out in Zimbabwe, where the printing presses could not keep up with the devaluation of that country's dollar.

If you convert your rands to US dollars today, it's probably because you believe that you will have greater buying power using American money five years from now than you will with rands. Over previous decades, you would have been proved correct. But it's impossible to predict the future. The reality is that the rand will weaken over time against the currencies of countries with lower inflation rates. There are periods when currencies either improve or weaken too much, but over the long term you should see currencies revert to long-term trends.

This is one of the reasons why the South African Reserve Bank operates on a mandate from the National Treasury to protect the currency and, amid all the prevailing economic and political turbulence, keep it as stable as possible by managing its value through raising and lowering interest rates.

Money is the lifeblood of society. The more you have, the wealthier you are, the more economic choices you can exercise. You can live in a better house in a better area, choose better schools for your kids, eat better food, go on better holidays, get better health care. Most importantly, money gives you more choices over your own destiny. Countries with strong currencies have more choices than countries with a weak exchange rate.

While a 'strong' currency has positive connotations, there are drawbacks. The stronger the rand, the less competitive the country's global exports and domestic labour. South Africa has low levels of labour productivity. If that improved, we could tolerate a considerably stronger currency.

One of the reasons China has grown so strongly for the past three decades is that its currency has been weak relative to the US dollar. China has become the world's factory and produces products for a fraction of the price of countries elsewhere. It has remained competitive because it has pegged its currency against the dollar, much to the annoyance of President Donald Trump. This is one of the key reasons behind the long-running trade dispute between the two countries. China is exercising an unfair advantage against its biggest customer in terms of trade through having a currency that is weaker than it should be.

Stability or at least an element of predictability is also important for a currency. That can only come in a stable policy environment, which South Africa has lacked for the better part of a decade. Uncertainty over property rights and the laws governing everything from pensions to the independence of the Reserve

Bank all contribute to uncertainty.

Modest amounts of inflation are generally helpful to grow economies. But shocks and uncontrolled devaluation like that seen in South Africa in 2000/1 cause havoc as they undermine consumer purchasing power and corrode confidence. Inflation erodes the value of money. In South Africa, which has a track record of higher inflation rates than many developed countries, it's not been unusual to see the purchasing power of the rand fall by more than 5% a year. When this is compounded, the ability of consumers to buy globally is seriously undermined and standards of living are negatively affected.

This is a primary reason why the Reserve Bank is mandated by National Treasury to keep inflation between 3% and 6%: not too hot and not too cold. If inflation rises, the Reserve Bank dampens demand by raising rates. If it drops, rates (theoretically) get cut to stimulate demand. The Reserve Bank's current hyper-cautious stance (due to the huge economic unknowns in the world) is doing little to help growth. But that is not the Reserve Bank governor's job. Lesetja Kganyago is paid his salary to maintain price stability in the present, but also to keep a beady eye out for future potential risks. As a result he and his committee will naturally err on the side of extreme caution.

South Africa is a big importer of global goods and services. Our current account depends on the value of our exports matching our imports. Not that it ever happens. Our dependency, for example, on crude oil imports for fuel means that a big chunk of our imports depends on the dollar price of oil and the value of our currency against that of the US dollar.

For those of you who like to remember the 1970s with more than just a pinch of nostalgia, when you could get two dollars for every rand, I should recall that the country then had a closed economy and demand for ZAR was practically nonexistent. The fortunes of the rand have long been tied to political events. Capital controls, for example, were ramped up in the 1960s following the Sharpeville massacre when, as is typical at times of uncertainty, outflows increased. The country instituted draconian controls and introduced the blocked rand system, preventing outflows through legal channels.

Controls eased towards the end of the 1970s but the financial rand was reintroduced during PW Botha's states of emergency in the mid-1980s when there were substantial capital outflows as a result of the economic sanctions imposed on the country. The fin-rand provided for a double exchange rate system: one for current account transactions and one for capital account transactions for non-residents. Foreigners could sell assets only for financial rand, which traded at a far worse rate than the rand itself. The measure was designed to discourage outflows of capital, but by this time sentiment against the apartheid state was so strong that few seemed to care about what losses they took as they ran for the door.

As the economy opened up after 1994 and the currency began trading freely on global markets, the rand went through a period of real depreciation, interspersed with periods of crisis. It also then became clear that it would not only be vulnerable to the vagaries of its own economy but also subjected to those of global events. The first wobble happened in 1996. In addition to a slowdown in the US and a crisis in Mexico, South Africa's Government of National Unity, led by Nelson Mandela, fell apart when FW de Klerk, the former National Party president, withdrew from the GNU. Markets began to bet against the ability of the ANC to run the economy. The fall was exacerbated by worries about Mandela's health and the appointment of Tito Mboweni as governor of the Reserve Bank. Mboweni, as it turned out, became a very effective central-bank governor and would serve two terms at the helm of the Bank. Currently he is fighting a rearguard action as finance minister to rescue the South African economy.

The Asian markets crisis of 1998 inflicted real damage on the value of the rand. Between the end of April and the end of August 1998, the rand depreciated by 28% against the US dollar. The Reserve Bank failed to understand the moves and spent its foreign reserves trying to defend the value of the rand. Interest rates shot up by around 700 basis points. Share prices collapsed by about 40% as the economy contracted. In 2001 there was also another period of sharp depreciation and the rand again shed more than a quarter of its value against the dollar. This crisis caught the small bank Sasfin off guard. It had to scramble to upgrade its live currency billboard on the side of the M1 South motorway in Johannesburg as the currency weakened for the first time ever beyond R10/$.

With the opening of the economy after sanctions were lifted and the ability of local firms to diversify globally for the first time, the value of the currency became dependent on flows in and out of the country. There was a gradual devaluation over time.

As the Reserve Bank grappled with this new unknown world, it moved twice to raise interest rates and ran down reserves to prevent weakness – and failed both times. But since the 2000s the Reserve Bank has concentrated on inflation targeting and no longer intervenes in the value of the rand.

The rand has become one of the most volatile currencies in the world. The dot-com bubble and burst, followed by 9/11 and regional worries about the collapse of Zimbabwe, precipitated another crisis. In response, the government appointed the Myburgh Commission of Inquiry and, while it failed to point to any particular reason for the currency collapse, it did contribute to a better understanding of its many vulnerabilities.

The early 2000s also provided some relief to the 'one-way bet' scenarios so popular at the time. Sasfin, having invested in a new digital currency billboard with place for four digits, would hardly need them again until the global financial crisis of 2008 when markets were once again thrown into turmoil and the rand began its weakening trend.

Do we obsess unnecessarily about its levels? No, says John Cairns, the currency strategist at RMB. 'Along with interest rates it is one of the key price levels in the economy, it's a major driver of inflation, and thus the interest-rate cycle.' The value of the currency does matter and cannot simply 'be picked up', as flippantly suggested by the former minister Nomvula Mokonyane, in defence of the economically inept Jacob Zuma administration soon after he had summarily fired Pravin Gordhan and Mcebisi Jonas, his finance minister and deputy respectively. This was the point at which ratings agency Standard & Poor's (S&P) lost patience and downgraded South Africa to junk, the first of the ratings agencies to do so. Moody's at that time put South Africa on negative ratings watch. It would later give South Africa breathing room after Zuma's sacking and, at the time of writing, was considering joining both S&P and Fitch to downgrade the country to sub-investment grade.

So the currency is critical. It is a key variable for business. It affects prices and therefore affects everyone, the poor most of all, as they are the most economically vulnerable members of society. The wealthy have historically operated counterintuitively. During periods of rand strength, they have kept their assets in local currency, while during bouts of weakness and, more often than not, close to the bottom, they have panicked out of the rand into so-called hard currency.

A board member of a respected JSE-listed company confided in me shortly after Gordhan and Jonas were fired that he'd taken money out of the country at R25/pound. He should have known better, he admitted, but he could no longer accept the uncertainty. This individual, who has been in financial markets all his life, panicked at precisely the wrong time, and his wealth was negatively affected as a result.

Could the rand ever return to single digits against the dollar? It seems unlikely considering the strong growth which the US economy has enjoyed in recent years relative to South Africa, whose economy has stuttered and faltered as a result of poor policies and toxic politics. A dramatic turnaround in the fortunes of the currency would require a significant improvement in the quality of South Africa's politics and policy-making, and the economy would need to be growing while the rest of the world grew too. That might also weaken the dollar and lift commodity prices. Such a scenario seems a little far-fetched in the short term.

Usually the rand is strong when the world is strong because both the country and the rand tend to be more positive when global conditions are supportive. But a weaker currency is also helpful, as the example of China, which we have already quoted, shows. A weaker rand helps producers at the expense of consumers, and supports growth. Back home, exporters such as the citrus farmers of the Sundays River Valley near Port Elizabeth and the avo and nut farmers of Mpumalanga are considerable beneficiaries of a weaker rand as it is good for their exports. As long as they are able to export competitively, they are able to keep employing and growing their local enterprises.

What's the ideal level for the rand against the US dollar? Probably around R13 right now, regardless of what *The Economist*'s Burgernomics survey will tell you when they compare the price of a Big Mac around the world. In terms of the purchasing-power parity of the world's most commonly sold burger, the rand could be closer to R7/$, but that would have devastating consequences for local export industries. The only way South Africa will be able to sustain a stronger currency is if it becomes a lot more productive, and productive countries tend to have better-than-average educated workforces and a multitude of other factors in their favour. It's not going to happen soon.

So back to my (now-) famous R1 coin, which sits on my laptop. It will buy me R1 worth of stuff. What if by some miracle my parents had deposited that R1 into a savings account and somehow secured a fixed 10% return for me in an account with zero fees? Between 1966 and now, the compounding effects should have been very favourable. What if, instead, they'd invested that money in the stock market? Or would the coin be worth more today if it had just sat in the back of a drawer for 54 years, thanks to its silver value of R250?

Let's do the maths.

R1 invested at 10% compounded over 54 years is worth R145 today. You would have had to earn a rate of 11.25% compounded annually to achieve the equivalent value of the coin. Over that time stock markets have risen by an average 19% a year compounded.

The answer to my puzzle is that the coin, thanks to its silver content, was worth more in the back of the drawer than in the bank over time.

My dad was a small boy in the Great Depression when an old man called Mr Kasimatis turned up at the farm gate looking for shelter. It was the mid-1930s and farmers were experiencing the worst drought in living memory. Mr Kasimatis was walking from Kroonstad to Klerksdorp, a distance of 117 kilometres, which even with today's potholed roads can be covered by car in an hour and a half. It was a different world back then. There was very little motorised traffic and he was having little luck at catching a ride. He needed shelter for the night. My grandfather gave him a blanket and let him sleep in an outbuilding. The next morning he gave my father and his twin brother each half-a-crown as a token of his gratitude.

The twins were resting on their beds after lunch and my father was admiring the way the coin glinted in the bright afternoon sunlight. My uncle had put his coin in a safe place. As my dad fantasised about the number of gob-stoppers (there wasn't much choice in those days) he could buy with the coin, it slipped from his hand, rolled across the wooden floor and slipped between the planks into the cavity below. It was gone. My dad pleaded with his father to rip up the floorboards to retrieve his treasure but he refused. It made no sense to do so. The damage it would cause outstripped the value of the coin.

'That will teach you,' he told my tearful father, all of seven or eight years old, 'never to play with money.' About 30 years later, when the old house was torn down, my father went to the spot in the corner of the room where the coin had slipped through the floor, inserted a crowbar and lifted the board. The coin was still there – worthless. South Africa was using the rand by then.

I have that coin in the back of a drawer. It won't ever be worth anything other than as a great prop to use to tell my kids why they should never play with money. Rather invest it in the stock market. After all, if my R1 coin had been put in the market on the day it was minted rather than left to gather dust, it would be worth R1,241 today.

CHAPTER 11

Blunders

'Time is a great teacher. Unfortunately it kills all its pupils.'
– Hector Berlioz

Robbie Brozin always seems to be in a good mood. The day I bumped into him at OR Tambo International Airport he was bounding about the place like Tigger in AA Milne's *Winnie-the-Pooh*. Most South Africans nowadays are more like Eeyore the donkey, for whom every silver lining has a cloud. So it's good to feed off Robbie's energy.

Brozin co-founded Nando's in 1987. The only thing hotter than his spicy chicken was the political climate. Brozin and his mate Fernando Duarte bought an out-of-the-way Portuguese restaurant in a poorer part of Johannesburg called Rosettenville. It served traditional Portuguese fare, but the chicken was exceptional. Brozin ran the business until 2010, then opted out as its global expansion took it beyond a thousand stores in more than 20 countries, including the US, UK, Bangladesh and Fiji. Its brilliance lies in the fact that its Portuguese branding does not position the firm as overtly South African: it's exotic but sufficiently aspirational to draw a diverse crowd all over the world. Like SAB, referred to by the venerable *Financial Times* as 'British brewer SABMiller' because of its London listing, Nando's is also regarded as part of the furniture in the UK. British comedians regularly use Nando's as a backdrop to the tales they tell. Not quite fine dining, not quite fast food – but a cool place to hang out and get a decent feed.

Brozin, who still curates the brand for the business, ensures that it stays true to its roots. There is a painting by a South African artist in every branch of Nando's in the world. It's part of the firm's corporate social investment and makes it the owner of probably the largest, though certainly not the most valuable, art collection in corporate South Africa.

When I met him at the airport, Brozin had just returned from Nigeria delivering mosquito nets for his NGO Goodbye Malaria with intrepid explorer Kingsley Holgate, and he was off to Mozambique in a couple of days to continue his mission to reduce malaria-infection rates across Africa.

Nando's is one of a handful of successful South African globalisations, backed with private money from the Enthoven family, owners of the Hollard insurance company, who don't court publicity. Most global expansions have been very public, eye-wateringly expensive and often disastrous. But amid the debris of shattered egos and failed dreams there have been some great successes. It's fair to say that without global diversification, investors on the JSE would not have harvested the sorts of returns they have enjoyed over the past quarter of a century.

The dawning of democracy and the international acceptance

of South Africa as an investment destination after decades of mounting sanctions, combined with the hunger of local companies for new investment and growth after being constrained for so long by apartheid, led to an explosion of opportunities.

Just as I stood outside the Manchester pub and marvelled at the coincidence of the SAB-owned beers, the Bidvest truck and Nando's outlet, it dawned on me that I needed to tap the brains of the founders of some of South Africa's great companies who were still around.

- How did three massively capable A-types keep it together in a business partnership that spanned 40 years to build a R450bn financial-services business?
- How did a CA whose wife in the early days used a forklift to move bags of rice from the garage to the pavement outside the family home create one of South Africa's biggest service companies?
- Could Christo Wiese retain his Midas touch? (This was a week before the Steinhoff implosion!)
- What was Raymond Ackerman's biggest regret in a lifetime of pioneering supermarketing in South Africa? Was it the failed ventures in Australia?
- Why did Australia become the graveyard for so many South African companies' global aspirations?
- Why was Adrian Gore so insistent on building a bank at a time of huge political pressure for nationalising the Reserve Bank and private capital?

And a whole lot more besides.

While there have been extraordinary global success stories of South African companies expanding internationally, there have also been serious failures costing shareholders hundreds of billions of rand. Sage was a venerable South African life assurer which took a big bet that it could compete in the US. It failed, and all that remains is a faint outline of a once-proud logo attached to its former head office, now a battered local-government building, in Sauer Street in downtown Johannesburg. Old Mutual spent stupid money on its ventures abroad but survived and would eventually unbundle the remaining fruits of its international expansion drive to return home, battered but still alive.

All too often, the common way in which South African companies made global acquisitions was that their quarry would see them coming. More often than not, they overpaid for bad companies that needed fixing. The most successful foreign investment ventures neither overpaid for nor bought other people's problems.

There is also the issue of local knowledge. Buying a company in your own backyard is complex enough, but buying one ten thousand miles away in a foreign jurisdiction is quite another matter. 'A source of undoing has often been a lack of depth of experience and relationships in the country or sector niche being expanded into,' says Meryl Pick, a retail-specialist fund manager at Old Mutual. 'For example, though the Woolworths group was experienced in Australian retail and in retail in general, it did not understand the demands of the department store subsector specifically. It went into a sector that had structural headwinds.'

SAB, by contrast, had a blueprint that worked. It expanded quickly first across the African continent and then into Eastern Europe as those economies opened up for business at the same time that rival Western European brewers also sought to get a foothold in new markets. Eastern bloc breweries had beloved but neglected beer brands and SAB was able to turn around these operations fairly quickly by doing simple things such as introducing new bottles and fresh branding and improving delivery systems.

The company became a substantial exporter of executive talent, as it put South Africans in charge of operations as it bought them up. Kevin Hedderwick, the executive hired by the immigrant Halamandaris family to grow their fledgling Steers takeaway burger business, from R60m to over R10bn by the time he retired, received his training at SAB and described it as the best MBA that money couldn't buy.

SAB emboldened other South African companies, which sought to emulate the brewer's success. The big difference was that SAB knew beer, and the people it trained ran operations like machines. There was no room for creativity and fancy tricks. It was all about sourcing raw materials, brewing beer, marketing the stuff, and getting it to market. SAB had been doing that for decades.

The problem with most acquisitions by South Africans is that they bought troubled businesses at tempting prices in the belief that they could turn them around. They have done this countless times and, observes the veteran fund manager Wayne McCurrie, sellers have seen them coming. Whether it was Old Mutual on its acquisition spree buying insurance companies across the globe in its failed quest for international dominance, or hospital groups Netcare and Mediclinic, or a host of retailers from Pick n Pay to Woolworths, or Steinhoff: South African companies in a desperate rush to diversify earnings streams from a perpetually precarious, politically fraught South African environment have wasted hundreds of billions of rand on failed ventures. Only a few have been successful.

Nampak, Shoprite and MTN have all suffered in recent years as a result of the Nigerian, Zimbabwean and Angolan economies taking strain with lower oil prices and foreign-exchange devaluations. Pepkor, a resilient operator and often early mover into new African markets, announced in late November 2019 that it would be withdrawing from Zimbabwe. If Pep is pulling out of a territory, you know it's doomed.

Brait, once a South African high-flyer like that other Christo Wiese-controlled business, Steinhoff, is also in trouble. It has become the subject of an embarrassing virtual takeover by rival Ethos, which announced it would be selling off the company's underlying assets over the next five years and returning the capital to shareholders, the biggest of whom is Wiese. Brait paid R37.5bn for fashion business New Look and quickly wrote its value down to zero, while other of its international businesses struggled too. To be fair, Brait was not alone in making poor acquisitions. Life has not been so good beyond South Africa's borders for the likes of Truworths with Office or Foschini with Phase Eight either.

At the prestigious Sunday Times Top 100 Awards in 2019, the three top-performing companies over the preceding five years were all firms that were wholly focused on operating in South Africa and had not fallen into the temptation of international expansion.

The best performer, Capitec, a business grown out of micro-lending in the early 2000s to a no-frills retail-banking operation with over 13 million customers served by a growing network of more than 850 branches, in a market where rivals are downsizing, has yet to show any interest in expanding outside the country.

An investment of R10,000 in Capitec shares in 2014 would have grown at a compound annual growth rate of 40.9% over that period, to be worth R55,491 in 2019. In fact, Capitec has been named top company an unprecedented four times in the past decade. In second place, Transaction Capital, owners of microlender Bayport and taxi-financing business SA Taxi, has grown by focusing on niche local industries, while Clicks was placed third.

Many domestic retailers have burned their investors by going global. It is therefore ironic that Clicks, a local retailer run by a foreigner, should be the best-performing retailer on the stock market. Clicks has been run until recently for more than a decade by ex-Boots executive David Kneale, who has focused on the domestic market, consolidating the group's dominance in the pharmacy market and incrementally growing a wholly South African retailer.

It's easy to blame executives for the billions that have been lost, but companies have come under pressure from shareholders, boards and even internally in recent years to diversify away from South Africa, which for many has carried too high a socio-political risk. For a lot of them, like Famous Brands, which paid a fortune for Gourmet Burger Kitchen before writing down a large part of its value, the deals seemed smart at the time. Why put all your investments in one jurisdiction, particularly one as vulnerable as South Africa, when you can diversify into stable currency environments? Then Brexit happened and Donald Trump was elected US president, sparking a trade war with the Chinese at a time of delicate imbalance in the state of play with foreign markets.

It's clear that neither management teams nor boards adequately weighed up all the risks involved. A myopic view of South African risk caused even bigger mistakes to be made. 'Whenever it was suggested to us that we expand into a new market, we always asked the same question: which member of the executive team wants to go and live there?' quips FirstRand co-founder Laurie Dippenaar. Invariably, he notes, there is not a business case to be made for a move, and it's often used as an excuse for a member of a team to relocate without the hassle of having to set up a whole new network. No doubt this has happened many times. Tellingly, over the past five years, despite the rise in tensions in the world of investing, the least-risky strategy has been to expand in home markets and known industries.

In markets as in life, size matters. If you bet the farm, it can break you. Sasol spent almost its entire market value on expansion at Lake Charles in Louisiana, where it set up a specialist ethane cracker plant. The project went over time and over budget, and the company was forced to gear up its balance sheet to fund the expansion. A report late in 2019 commissioned by the board laid the blame squarely at the feet of the executives and said they should take the fall. The firm's joint CEOs each walked away amid concerns that the top-down culture of the organisation had made it impossible for bad news to travel up the chain of command. By the time HQ in Sandton became aware there was a problem, the damage was done.

'The list of clear success is far shorter than the list of clear failure, and there are many more that are muddling through but for now appear to have destroyed value,' says Old Mutual's Meryl Pick. She notes that many of the successes internationally have emerged from the Ruperts' Rembrandt empire or the Anglo American stable: British American Tobacco, Richemont, Mondi and SAB are all legendary success stories as is the expansion of Bidcorp and, of course, Naspers, whose fortuitous acquisition of a stake in an unknown gaming firm called Tencent less than 20 years ago fundamentally altered its business model and trajectory. Barloworld is another firm which expanded globally in the early 2000s, but it really only succeeded in Russia.

MTN, under the visionary leadership of Phuthuma Nhleko, has had the most successful African expansion of any company on the JSE. Over the past five years or so the MTN share price has been under pressure, as the company has had to grapple with multiple issues, most notably its regulatory battles in Nigeria and its difficulty in getting money out of some of its markets. South Africa makes up about 30% of MTN group revenue. More recently, its Middle East operations have proved to be a drag, not to mention the massive administrative sanctions applied to its business in Nigeria, which was separately listed on the Nigerian Stock Exchange in 2019.

The failures are the most interesting part. Which are the really big ones? Why did they fail?

Woolies has so far written off about R20bn (and counting) on David Jones in Australia. The company, an ageing Australian department-store operator, was the group's big foray Down Under. This disastrous acquisition was made on the watch of Ian Moir, the Scottish-born retailer who was hired in 2010 from Country Road in Australia to run Woolworths out of Cape Town. At the time, the South African business was faring well. It was, as it always is, a bit hit and miss on clothing and it never really got a firm-enough grip on its interior-decorating lines to have a massive impact on its earnings. It was the food business that was the real star in the group. Woolworths had succeeded in differentiating itself in the South African business environment by positioning itself as the custodian of good food. It created meaningful tie-ups with local farmers who became exclusive suppliers of superlative-quality fresh produce, and it was able to charge a premium based on its brand presence in the local market.

Shareholders were, however, keen on diversification. Woolies served upper-income shoppers in a market that was not really creating enough new wealth to provide an organically growing customer set that would satisfy the shareholders' rapacious sense of what they deserved in terms of returns. So they and the board were constantly challenging the management team to find hard-currency earnings. Moir knew the Australian market well. It was the country he considered home, and when David Jones came on the market Moir went into a bidding war and disastrously overpaid. The price tag of R21.5bn was immediately criticised.

It also quickly became clear that without a swift and creative turnaround strategy for a business that would devour capital as it sought to build its franchise, it would lose lots of money.

And it did. Fund manager Evan Walker at 36ONE Asset Management has looked at the opportunity cost of tying up so much capital in a dying business and says it makes the impact of poor management decisions even worse: 'It comes to about R15bn in lost returns, and that puts the write-offs they have taken in context.' Woolworths, once a staple holding in any long-term investor's portfolio, has lost the trust of the investing public.

How did it get it so wrong? The company admits as much in its annual report, blaming 'poor execution of key initiatives' as well as spiralling costs and significant disruption as a result of the drawn-out refurbishment of its flagship Sydney store. The advent of online shopping, which has caught out so many South African retailers entering new markets, particularly in the UK, has meant that the businesses that have been acquired are no longer fit for purpose.

Moir admitted to news agency Bloomberg in a mid-2019 interview that he'd overpaid for David Jones, telling the service: 'I regret the price, and buying it at that time – hindsight is a wonderful thing – but I think we have a great asset now.' Tell that to shareholders, who can't sell the share for anything close to what they paid for it in 2014.

In the two years after the deal, Moir earned over R100m in his job. That has been reduced over time. So in 2015 he was paid R49m; in 2016 his earnings peaked and he pulled in R53.8m; but those payments decreased in subsequent years to R34.7m,

R30.8m and R23m. The company is on the hunt for his replacement. In the meantime he has been tasked with turning around the mess in Australia.

Other companies that have similarly burned their fingers overseas have also suffered significant losses. Brait wrote down the entire purchase price of New Look, while Tiger Brands lost R850m on a deal with Africa's richest man, Aliko Dangote. Mediclinic wrote off R8.1bn on Hirslanden in Switzerland and Spire in the UK, while Netcare is still trying to extricate itself from the remnants of its UK business, which started with an enormous expectation that the British government, unable to serve all the patients who attended NHS facilities, would therefore need access to easily available private care. The numbers never really added up. Sasol cannot be absolutely certain that it is done paying for its ethane cracker plant in Louisiana, and costs may continue to pile up there.

And it's not just about the money; it's also about opportunity cost. Global expansions take up a significant amount of executive time, energy and focus. While Pick n Pay was trying on two occasions to venture into Australia, its competitors were building massive distribution centres back home and ensuring they could get their products to domestic shoppers. Tiger Brands must have taken its eye off the ball and made too little investment in its South African business as it battled to fix its investment in Dangote Flour Mills in Nigeria. Many South African companies have been humbled in that country, including even the mighty KFC, which eventually closed up shop.

The real cost to investors as a result of the global jaunts is mind-boggling. Mediclinic, a great local brand, has seen its value fall 69%. Woolworths has underperformed on the JSE All Share Index (ALSI) by 34% since August 2014 when the David Jones deal was concluded. Tiger Brands has lost very nearly half its value since it acquired Dangote. Brait has underperformed on the ALSI by 85% since acquiring New Look, and Steinhoff is down 99% from its peak and is holding on for dear life.

Which has been the best-performing retailer over the past ten years? My sense is that Clicks would be there or thereabouts. Interestingly, it's one of the few companies that did not go gallivanting globally. Likewise, Mr Price, another successful local retailer, tested Australia but had the good sense, like Discovery in the US, to abandon the project before it did permanent damage. Relative to ALSI, Clicks has done 341% over ten years. Mr Price has outperformed ALSI by 156% over the same period.

The problem is that South Africa is seen by many to be ex-growth, and that's why many companies have taken the approach to sell down their investments. It's high time that local companies shifted their spending priorities and did more domestic investment and halt the inevitability of a likely downgrade. As Johann Rupert, probably one of the five most successful executives in diversifying his wealth globally, said in a rare radio interview on Power FM: 'Before foreigners invest in South Africa, they would look at us if we invest.'

Domestically, there is the view that South Africa is too risky a place to invest in and that offshore investing is good for diversification. And we see ordinary investors following the same logic: offshore wealth at any cost, at any exchange rate, all out of fear.

In hindsight, many South African companies that have been

successful locally have benefited from limited competition, a relatively closed economy over most of their history, and a government-subsidised boom in consumer spending over the last 20 years, due to the growth in social grants and in the civil service.

The benefit of restricted competition is illustrated by short-term insurer Santam, which has compounded its share price at 18% a year (excluding dividends) from the beginning of 1985 until now. Headline inflation averaged 8% a year over this period. This return is particularly impressive when you consider that Santam has been primarily a domestic-focused company. Between 1985 and today, South Africa witnessed the Rubicon speech, narrowly avoided a civil war, weathered four technical recessions, and suffered through 86 months in which the year-on-year decline in the rand was more than 20%. Despite all this, Santam's ability to withstand competition and retain its market share has gone from strength to strength. Because South Africa has not been viewed as an attractive place to do business, there has been little competition from international heavyweights. This has allowed Santam to build scale and make itself increasingly tough to compete with.

Many management teams have underestimated how relatively easy they have it in South Africa, particularly when it comes to limited competition. In doing so, they in turn underestimate how difficult offshore markets can be, where they will face considerably more competition.

Back to the effervescent Robbie Brozin.

'The world's fucked, hey!' Brozin said, as he bounded over to me with characteristic energy. He was referring to how unsettled geopolitics have become, the subtext being that South Africa, for all its problems, is fixable if one has the right approach.

'If you quote me, make sure you do it properly.' And off he went, pleased with himself and the world around him. Robbie, your wish is my command.

CHAPTER 12

· · · · · · · · · · · · ·

Champagne tastes with beer money

'This isn't life in the fast lane, it's life in the oncoming traffic.'
– Terry Pratchett

The only thing better than a State of the Nation Address to assess the well-being of an economy is the country's budget speech. Speeches themselves are deceptive, though, and that's why the government likes to broadcast its messages far and wide. The country comes to a halt as citizens hang on every word, seeking inspiration for the future. At least, that's what politicians seem to think we do. In my job, I have to pay attention, then summarise the content into digestible titbits.

Poring over budget documents, locked up in parliamentary meeting rooms in the hours before the finance minister and his team take a walk down Parliament Avenue to deliver the annual address, I have become aware from year to year of the slow burn of government finances and the deterioration of the fiscus. South Africa could soon test the Dornbusch rule. Commenting on the Mexico crisis of the early 1990s, economist and Latin America expert Rudi Dornbusch observed 'a crisis takes a much longer time coming than you think, and then it happens much faster than you would have thought'. It's a warning to the Ramaphosa administration that the time for tinkering on the periphery of South Africa's myriad problems, is over, unless they want to be at the bridge when all hell breaks loose.

Over the years hard-working Treasury officials, on hand to answer questions about any detail tucked into the reams of budget documents, have become increasingly morose as they realise that the politicians do not have the slightest idea of just how serious the country's financial position is.

It was either 2011 or 2012, and Pravin Gordhan was finance minister. Konrad Reuss, the long-serving managing director of S&P Global, one of three international ratings agencies that the country pays to evaluate its international creditworthiness, delivered a withering assessment of the country's fiscal path. We were spending too much and earning too little, he said. We needed to start cutting back on expenditure and driving growth, otherwise we would get to a point where we lost the right to manage our own finances. Gordhan, on the phone from parliament after a tough week of trying to formulate the most palatable version of the budget, was furious and launched a stinging personal attack on Reuss. The exact phrasing of his response escapes me. But it was biting and personal and came down to this: if Reuss doesn't like the way we are running the country, then why does he live here?

On the Monday immediately after the most recent ratings assessment from S&P, in November 2019, I once again had Konrad Reuss in the studio to explain why they were preparing to take

South Africa even deeper into sub-investment grade. S&P, the first ratings agency to downgrade South Africa to junk since 1999, was turning increasingly negative about the country's ability to resolve its own problems. Like Moody's, which just weeks before had retained an investment grade for South Africa but put the country on a negative outlook, S&P remained convinced that things would get worse before they got better. Moody's had been scathing in its analysis of President Cyril Ramaphosa's 'lack of political capital' to drive the economic-reform agenda he knows he must deliver in order to prevent the inevitable downgrade.

South Africa had been spending too much for too long in anticipation of growth which never materialised. In fact it was never going to. Money was going to all the wrong places. The public-sector wage bill was expanding at a rate higher than inflation, and the number of people employed in government service was expanding without the necessary productivity gains such appointments should bring. The state was less and less capable, several government departments were being 'captured', and money was being stolen at an alarming rate. The full extent of that looting would only become apparent following the ousting of Jacob Zuma and the implementation of a series of commissions of inquiry.

I reminded Konrad Reuss about our previous studio meeting. He remembered it clearly.

'You were right,' I said.

'I was,' he replied, without an ounce of satisfaction.

Still, the government persists with pipe dreams dressed up as economic strategy. Fresh from his May 2019 election victory, albeit with a reduced majority, Cyril Ramaphosa presented his first State of the Nation Address as elected president to an expectant country. His first SONA had been a bland affair just days after the ousting of Jacob Zuma in February 2018. The second took place a year later, once the so-called Ramaphoria effect had worn off and there was an uneasy sense of Ramareality.

Whether he was seeking to invoke the spirit of JFK's 'we will go to the moon in this decade, not because it is easy, but because it is hard', or whether he was motivated by the drive, energy and success of fast-growing post-apocalyptic Rwanda, is not clear. Ramaphosa said many things that night. It is plain he understood the real tragedy of being born poor in South Africa and being trapped in economic circumstances from which there is very little chance of escape. But the nation mainly focused on the president's vision. He promised all the usual stuff that politicians say but don't really mean because they are unsure about where to start: fixing crime, creating jobs – just platitudes really.

And then he launched into the vision. A vision is a good thing – but the people you are sharing it with need to believe you to make it work. The big difference between JFK's moon speech and Ramaphosa's smart-cities-and-bullet-trains speech is that America was riding on the crest of a wave of optimism following a decade of solid post-war growth, whereas Ramaphosa was trying to lift a country out of the depths of despair.

'We also want a South Africa where we stretch our capacities to the fullest as we advance along the super-highway of progress. We want a South Africa that has prioritised its rail networks, and is producing high-speed trains connecting our megacities and the remotest areas of our country. We should imagine a country where bullet trains pass through Johannesburg as they travel from here to Musina, and they stop in Buffalo City on their way from eThekwini back here. We want a South Africa with a high-tech economy where advances in e-health, robotics and remote medicine are applied as we roll out the National Health Insurance. We want a South Africa that doesn't simply export its raw materials but has become a manufacturing hub for key components used in electronics, in automobiles and in computers. We must be a country that can feed itself and that harnesses the latest advances in smart agriculture. I dream of a South Africa where the first entirely new city built in the democratic era rises, with skyscrapers, schools, universities, hospitals and factories,' he said. 'Has the time not arrived for us to be bold and reach beyond ourselves and do what may seem impossible? Has the time not arrived to build a new smart city founded on the technologies of the 4th Industrial Revolution? I would like to invite South Africans to begin imagining this prospect.'

The speech was big, bold, audacious – and simply so far beyond the wildest imaginings of most South Africans that it fell horribly flat.

Usually after a SONA, government ministers retreat to their respective departments, apparently oblivious to their budgetary constraints, and concoct the most extraordinary plans to fix the particular crisis over which they preside. The Department of Health is yet to provide a plausible costing on National Health Insurance (NHI) but is barrelling ahead with plans for its implementation by 2026, regardless of any fiscal consequences. For the incumbent minister Zweli Mkhize, who inherited the NHI from his predecessor Aaron Motsoaledi, there is too big a personal political risk to cancel the plan regardless of whether it's feasible or not. It's almost as if ministers have to pursue departmental agendas until told by Treasury that it's a no-go so they can have someone else to blame. It makes Treasury as the last line of defence very unpopular in government, as it's the one department constantly having to say no.

No rational person wants a dysfunctional public health service. With medical inflation doubling the cost of private insurance every five years, the current funding model is unsustainable and cracks are already appearing for companies like Discovery which are seeing customers either cancel or trade down on cover. Government has to find a way to make the public health sector work better, and frankly it comes down to making sure people do their jobs better. As with public education, simply getting people to turn up and do their jobs would be the first battle won. The public service has more of a mindset problem than it does any other. Perhaps the inevitable cutting down on some public-sector jobs would focus the minds of those left behind a little more keenly.

Land reform remains high on the ANC's policy agenda. The government's failure to implement the party's 2017 resolution on redistribution without compensation could hurt the Ramaphosa administration. No amount of logic and evidence will divert individual interests masquerading as policy. Government's new approach to land reform, which looks to distribute state-owned land as a first step towards restitution, is a good start. It understands that Zimbabwe-style confiscation is a recipe for disaster and it is looking at compromises that will deliver fair outcomes for those who want a stake in the country's future but cannot afford to buy one. Its approach has high-level buy-in from the agricultural sector, and many large-scale farmers have gone into successful partnerships with black farmers as a way of finding sustainable solutions to seemingly intractable problems. Again, what is involved is a slow and agonising process for people who've been made promises that the future will be better than the past but who are yet to see tangible evidence of this.

'We have to stop trying to boil the ocean,' says Kenny Fihla, CEO of Standard Bank's Corporate and Investment Banking division. It's a great analogy. In pretending to fix everything, we tackle nothing. The problems are too big and too numerous to solve all at once.

There is mounting frustration in corporate South Africa about the difficulties of executing the government's big-picture goals. The National Development Plan was workable but has turned into a dead duck through a lack of focus and buy-in. Implementation of the NDP should be part of every minister's performance measures and they should be fired if they fail. But governments like weighty documents that are the work of multiple stakeholders; they like big plans. They like to present themselves as visionaries. And that's where it all falls flat. They are trying to boil the ocean.

When she was elected president of Liberia, the first woman in history to lead an African country, Ellen Johnson Sirleaf set herself and her government a series of short-term, highly achievable goals. Anything that demonstrated action was on the table. Whether it be tackling streetlights or traffic lights, lines painted on the roads or accurate street signage, it was all up for disruption

– but with clear guidance and control.

'It's important,' says Dr Adrian Saville, founder of Cannon Asset Managers, 'to set highly-achievable, short-term, measurable goals. Hundred-day goals work well. They demonstrate action. Those actions represent short-term wins. And especially when you are coming out of a dark place, you need evidence of victory. Even when those wins are modest, they are wins. And that is when you get the flywheel turning, and momentum builds.'

Imagine the mayors of South Africa's major metropolitan areas being set a task of repairing streetlights, for example; being given a realistic deadline and then being monitored at the end of that period to assess their success rate. And imagine that the success rate, good or bad, once independently verified, was posted in a prominent place for citizens to see: a massive hoarding across the M1 motorway in Johannesburg, for example, or along the N1 highway into Cape Town. Just to ensure the job was done properly, the same monitoring could take place on an annual basis.

'There is a lot of evidence that suggests that single policies with single visions would do well by trying a couple of things rather than being convinced by a single large vision which would be unachievable and impossible to measure,' says Saville.

Probably the most damaging result of South Africa's loss of prestige has been our collective loss of self-confidence. There was a time when nothing felt impossible. The gang-buster attitude of the Mandela and Mbeki eras, when South Africa was boxing far above its weight in international affairs, and when its companies were expanding globally and rapidly becoming adverts for the country's superlative financial system, market regulation and ability to perform at a high standard, has all but evaporated. Now nothing feels possible.

By the time Jacob Zuma headed the South African delegation to the World Economic Forum gathering at Davos in Switzerland in January 2016, the writing was on the wall. South Africa, still a drawcard just a year before, was no longer of any interest. The new Argentinian president was getting plenty of attention, as was the delegation from Iran. Optimism about prospects for their turnaround was short-lived, but everyone likes positive stories and the crowds flocked to learn what was going on. South Africa turned up in Davos just weeks after Nhlanhla Nene's sacking. The smiles were forced. The country was on a precipice and the South African delegates were trying valiantly to pretend it was business as usual – as much for themselves as for the rest of the world. The only problem was that the world was not biting.

Matters escalated when Zuma failed to turn up at a breakfast panel discussion that it had been confirmed he would attend weeks before. It was the Africa showcase panel, but he must have known the game was up. There was no way a panel discussion on future prospects for Africa could be held with the South African president present, without his facing extremely awkward questions about his increasingly erratic management of the state.

By this point, the Nkandla scandal was in full swing. The Waterkloof air-force base landing, which brought hundreds of guests from India to attend a Gupta family wedding, had happened three years before and it was apparent that the president was being played like a cheap banjo. Everyone knew that he was under pressure to sign a nuclear deal with Russia that the country could not afford, and all the while the ANC was covering for its president to the detriment of the country. It was factional politics at their most toxic.

South Africa had been subjected to the amateur-hour antics of the fire-pool debacle six months before, as the government frantically tried to defend its spending of R246m in taxpayers' money on a sitting president's rural retreat. As it turns out, that was chump change compared to the immeasurable looting of the fiscus that was then taking place, unbeknown to the South African public, across government departments and state-owned enterprises.

In previous years, the Africa panel had seen snaking lines as delegates queued to hear about the opportunities that the continent presented. This time round there were empty seats.

It was worse at Team South Africa's HQ at the Kirchner Museum in the middle of Davos. This occupies a prime spot just below the plush Belvedere Hotel, between the massive purpose-built conference centre and the village's main street filled with boutiques, bars and restaurants serving local delicacies like horse meat and rich, flaming fondue bowls. The place was like a morgue. Team South Africa was scrambling, and I was asked if I would chair a panel on the strength and resilience of the South African financial-services sector and the efficacy of its banking-sector regulations, which had so effectively protected the country from the worst fallout of the global financial crisis. Nobody turned up, and at 2.15 pm, a full 15 minutes after we were due to start, Reserve Bank governor Lesetja Kganyago called it a day.

That night there was a cocktail party rather than the traditional dinner. It may have been due to a budget constraint, or maybe there was a concern that if you sat delegates round a table, it would be easier to spot the gaps. There in the middle of the room was a pitiful semicircle of government ministers looking as if they would rather undergo root-canal surgery than be present in the room at that moment. Jeff Radebe, then Minister in the Presidency, Rob Davies at Trade and Industry, and Ebrahim Patel at Economic Development stood awkwardly cradling half-empty drinks with no one to talk to.

In the far corner Pravin Gordhan held court, cheering up the South African business delegation and getting them on board to create a business grouping that it was hoped would for the first time become more actively engaged in the political economy. The country was going to the wall. Gordhan knew it; the business leaders knew it. And they knew they had no choice but to present a united face on their return home and work together to improve the economy. Without this, they were doomed.

It was at Davos in 1992 that Nelson Mandela led an ANC delegation to the gathering of the world's most influential political and business leaders, and he was told in no uncertain terms that if he wanted foreign investment he would need to ensure his future government adopted free-market principles. The basic tone of the gathering was: it's your country and you can apply whatever economic model you see fit, but that choice will determine the choices that international investors make when considering where to apply their capital.

That week in Davos in 2016 was another critical turning point for South Africa when big business finally woke up to the fact that it could no longer just focus on creating shareholder value.

You cannot run a globally competitive company in a dysfunctional environment. Davos 2016 led to the creation of the CEO Initiative, and big business developed a united voice to make a contribution to the future of the country.

From that came the R1.4bn SA SME Fund. By September 2019 it had disbursed the funds to eight venture-capital firms with the requirement of investing the money in growth businesses that create jobs. In a country as hungry for capital as it is for great ideas, it will have a positive impact in creating an environment ripe for investible ideas. The fund has just embarked on a new capital-raising drive for more investments.

It turns out that Davos 2016 wasn't a complete waste of time after all.

By 2018, Zuma had given up attending the gathering at Davos. He'd just been replaced as party leader at a fractious elective conference by his deputy, Cyril Ramaphosa. Ramaphosa had won the leadership of the party by the narrowest of margins and used his first international visit as president-in-waiting to gauge international reaction. It was overwhelmingly positive. South Africa finally did have a good story to tell. Business delegates thanked their lucky stars that Nkosazana Dlamini-Zuma, regarded as a proxy for the sitting president (her ex-husband), had not been elected by the party. Such a step would have extended the country's pain and given more time for the looting of what was left of the fiscus.

Then followed the period of Ramaphoria. The currency began strengthening, the stock market rising towards record levels, and once again anything seemed possible. But it didn't last long. No sooner did Ramaphosa succeed in convincing his party to oust

Jacob Zuma than the factionalism of the party turned on him, stymieing any hope of a radical policy overhaul that would set the country on a sustainable growth path.

If only those blocking the reforms could fully comprehend that their actions are akin to turkeys each year voting for Christmas. It will lead to their inevitable demise but they know no other way to exist, so they keep doing the same thing over and over again, to their own detriment.

Fast forward to Davos 2020 and South Africa's underwhelming showing at the World Economic Forum (WEF), which had rapturously welcomed Ramaphosa in previous years. He must have known it would be a damp squib, or worse, that he might be challenged for failing to deliver on the myriad promises made to delegates at the gathering on his two recent visits.

South Africa had lost the prime Kirchner Museum venue to Facebook. Team South Africa had stationed itself at a local pizza joint called Restaurant Excellent, located about as far from the epicentre of Davos life as you can get without actually ending up on a ski slope or in a cow barn. A handful of foreign investors turned up to an intimate catch-up session on the Wednesday morning, where the financial director of Heineken told Tito Mboweni: 'Your power cuts really hurt us.' It was a frank gathering of the faithful, each spelling out the same concerns: worries about the safety of executives, water quality, electricity, governance, policy. 'You can't do stop-start policy changes all the time,' said one. Mboweni acknowledged their concerns, admitted they were right, and asked for patience. There were no new or prospective investors bashing down the door to get in.

In a short video interview I conducted with CNN host Richard Quest, which went viral in the days after the WEF event, he was highly critical of the country's lack of progress and summed up the poor showing. Quest is a regular traveller to South Africa and takes a deep interest in the story of the country: long on promises, short on delivery. I had preceded the interview with a question as to why he was not profiling South Africa in 2020 as he previously had, and he was clear: '… there's no point in coming here to say invest, invest, invest in me if you don't have the policies to back it up.' He referred to Pravin Gordhan's admission that state capture is probably worse than anyone could imagine. 'How many people have gone to prison so far?' Quest boomed, and in response to a question on the credibility of the Ramaphosa administration: 'What credibility?' It was a damning indictment of an administration that had allowed itself to become mired in its own politics and had forgotten its core purpose.

On Valentine's eve 2020, there was little love lost in parliament as Cyril Ramaphosa, warned that his annual State of the Nation Address would be disrupted unless he fired his Public Enterprises Minister Pravin Gordhan ahead of time, fumed as Julius Malema's EFF wrought havoc with parliamentary procedure. The EFF has made numerous spurious and often-racist attacks against Gordhan, who is at the forefront of trying to restore order inside a crippled state. Once the antics had been exhausted and, about 90 minutes late, the president delivered some key plans for the future. The plans, however, landed badly. In an economy as threadbare as South Africa's, the dream of a high-tech city at Lanseria has merit – but it must be enabled by the state and developed by private-sector players with sufficient confidence in the future to make the substantial financial commitment that will be required to deliver it. Pie-in-the-sky ideas included the development of a state bank, in a country that already has four agencies it could either adapt or amalgamate to achieve its goal. Postbank would be a logical place to start. The creation of a brand-new entity to compete with commercial banks is an accident waiting to happen. Banking is a risk game not a political one. The notion of a sovereign wealth fund any time soon for South Africa is startlingly tone deaf. It may be a pipe dream created in a Luthuli House session to emulate the massive success of, amongst others, oil-rich Middle Eastern economies or the highly productive Chinese state, but until South Africa produces more than it consumes, frankly it does not have the muscle to contemplate it.

For all his warmth, personal charm and many positive attributes, the State of the Nation was delivered by a billionaire president speaking like a trust-fund kid to his university classmates wondering why they are going to be doing holiday jobs over December rather than joining him in St Moritz for his annual ski break.

It might have been designed to sound progressive. It just sounded out of touch.

In a country where more than 10 million people – 10,000,000 people (it looks scarier that way) – cannot find work, please come up with a way to empower the small enterprises to flourish in a certain, peaceful and prosperous environment, which will create the jobs that government keeps talking about.

Conclusion

'In the long term, we are all dead.' – John Maynard Keynes

**Final question: What's the definition of an optimist in South Africa?
Answer: Someone who looks both ways before crossing a one-way street.**

That is our reality. South Africa is a place where red traffic lights are a suggestion, where the lane on the other side of the yellow line is yours if you are in a hurry or just too self-important to wait in the traffic jam with the rest of us, and where far too many of its citizens feel that the rules can be broken in the name of naked self-interest. It is also a place of extraordinary selflessness where women, in particular, take on the burden of raising families, where organisations like Gift of the Givers and thousands like them step into the breach to alleviate the worst extremes of human hardship as more and more people are betrayed by a failing state. It is the place that has produced a world-leading constitution, which has acted as an ever-present guardian through the darkest years of state capture. It is a place that produces globally competitive businesses, extraordinary sports teams, a disproportionate number of Miss Universe winners, and is home to a new generation of problem-solvers.

Whether your name is Stacey Brewer or Aisha Pandor and you are already on track to fundamentally change the world, or whether you are UCT biology dropout Alexandria Procter, who hit upon the idea of creating the equivalent of Airbnb for students in the form of digsconnect.com to help alleviate accommodation shortages, or the madly persistent Miles Kubheka, who has evolved into an acclaimed chef from being a character in a series of beer adverts for Hansa around the time of the 2010 Soccer World Cup, you are in fine company.

One also has to recognise the generation of immigrants who have made South Africa their home and are building businesses here for global application. There's Serge Raemaekers from Belgium whose Abalobi app is, as we have seen, connecting fishing communities to markets just as Aisha Pandor's SweepSouth connects people to jobs. It not only helps chefs source the best and freshest fish from along South Africa's coastline, but it also creates a connection between diners and fishermen, and a connection between the source of the food and the plate.

I should also mention the guy who arrived in South Africa to help set up global call centres but, after the frustration of dealing with regulators and after two heart attacks, decided to farm flies for a living instead. Today Jason Drew runs a Western Cape business called AgriProtein, based on the principle that fly larvae are a natural food for much of what we eat and can be farmed, processed and delivered in bulk as a natural alternative in an increasingly compromised food chain. The business has gone from a single experimental farm at Elsenburg near Stellenbosch in 2010 to multiple facilities today with tie-ups with serious researchers in that university town and in Texas as they explore new ways of reducing the environmental impact of the human production and disposal of food. As the world heads inexorably to a population of 10 billion by 2050, the problem of how to feed them while preserving the environment looms.

What do all these entities have in common beyond the fact that they all individually seek to solve problems? None of them existed ten years ago. These are businesses that were either started during or in the immediate aftermath of the 'lost decade' so intimately associated with the state-capture project.

That's the difference between 'them' and the rest. Those who see opportunity and create sustainable businesses do not ignore risk, and they create madcap ventures at the drop of a hat. They are able to critically assess risk and weigh it up against the opportunity they see and, crucially, act on their ideas. How often have you seen a business, sampled a product or service, and exclaimed: 'I thought of this years ago' or 'I could have done that!' The biggest difference is that they did it – you didn't.

Adrian Gore didn't wait for policy certainty in the medical-aid arena or certainty that there would be sufficient private hospitals to absorb enough people who would buy his particular insurance in an ocean of failing rivals. He made some astute assumptions about what the future would probably look like and what its needs might be. He was able to foresee as early as 1992 that there would probably be a political solution in South Africa and a transition to democracy, and on the other side of that would be a country that had underinvested in medical facilities. Those who had jobs would, he reckoned, need an insurance product to fund the private care for which many people would be willing to pay to protect themselves against what would become an overburdened public system.

Capitec founder Michiel le Roux understood there was a vast market of people deemed unbankable by the establishment players. Despite the small-banks crisis of the early 2000s as a result of failures of risk management, he persisted and developed a bank that now has over 13 million customers and has been one of the best-performing shares in the world over its short lifetime. Between December 2014 and December 2019, Capitec saw a 429% return, beaten by global new-economy businesses like AI firm Nvidia, Netflix and the mighty Amazon – but it's in fine company. Capitec has delivered twice the return of Naspers over the same period and nearly four times the return of South Africa's best-performing big-banking group, FirstRand. Capitec found a reason to exist and slavishly served its core market, focusing entirely on the domestic banking environment. It was named 'best bank in the world' for three years running in a survey run by Lafferty and later by US business magazine *Forbes*.

Aspen Pharmacare has had to sell some of its international businesses in order to reduce its debt after years of global expansion, but it remains globally diverse and a significant player in the pharmaceutical world. Anglo American and the country's platinum producers are world leaders. Richemont is one of the biggest luxury goods groups in the world and is connected through the Ruperts to British American Tobacco.

There are many other examples of successful world businesses emanating from South Africa. The name De Beers remains synonymous with diamonds, while in Asia Tencent, funded in the early days by an investment by the Cape Town newspaper group Naspers, fundamentally changed Naspers' own destiny and the future of the Chinese company too. Chairman Koos Bekker had the good idea to expect rapid growth in China, but not even he anticipated just how important a player Tencent would become in the domestic economy.

Massmart founder Mark Lamberti looked at the global trend of supermarketing, which was already dominated in South Africa by a handful of big retailers, and took a different path into warehouse shopping. He began harvesting consumer data by forcing customers to have Makro membership cards long before the rest of the trade knew what data was. In the same way that Raymond Ackerman was able to read global trends long before they arrived on South Africa's shores, Christo Wiese saw trends in value retail and would develop Pep and, later, Shoprite, and grow those businesses to serve consumers across Africa because he, like a handful of others, dared to think differently about solutions to the problems that the industry faced. When the first investors pondered the prospects for South Africa's mobile-telecommunications industry, they had no way of forecasting the digital revolution and the potential impact it could have on Africa in the future.

If you look at the environment into which all these entrepreneurs were preparing to launch their businesses, one would think they needed their heads read. There was no certainty; there was no 'positive outlook'. For most of them, South Africa was deep in junk status when they were founded. There was no good news to buoy them. They just started.

On the other hand, there was an opportunity and very little competition to derail their plans. They all wanted to do well. But none expected that the businesses they built would ever become the dominant forces that they have grown into. They could not have anticipated the surge in goodwill that accompanied South Africa's transition to democracy and the growth that followed the 1994 settlement. Indeed, the country could have gone either way. It could have regressed even further from the broken state in which the National Party left it, or it could have flourished, as it did under Mandela. His leadership not only paid attention to the counsel of global players as South African businesses entered an unprecedented period of global expansion, but also made it possible for them to make a profit. It's just a pity that the country didn't do more to keep pace with the way in which the world was changing. China and other Asian economies did, and many grew themselves out of poverty and inequality and became industrial players in a relatively short period of time. For individuals who saw opportunity, they coupled that with an obsessive attention to detail and they convinced others to do the real work of running the day-to-day operations while they freed themselves to think about growth and how to develop their ideas into globally competitive businesses.

We sit on the brink of another massive opportunity. Like most opportunities, it must either be seized or future generations will have to deal with our failure to capitalise on the chance for growth right now.

Many South African companies have expanded beyond South

Africa's borders into Africa, with varying degrees of success. Despite running into regulatory obstacles in some of its markets after its extraordinary expansion drive across Africa and into the Middle East, MTN is the gold standard for local firms seizing the Africa opportunity. At one point Shoprite sold more bottles of Moët & Chandon champagne at five stores in Nigeria in a year than across its entire network in South Africa, but that economy slowed dramatically in line with falling oil prices, thereby illustrating the dependence of so many countries on single commodity exports. Firms like Nampak have come unstuck in trying to repatriate funds from Angola and elsewhere, and that has dented many an executive's appetite for the continent.

In addition to its ill-fated UK expansion, Famous Brands has tried multiple ventures in many African countries and KFC famously signed up former Nigerian president Olusegun Obasanjo as its primary chicken supplier in that country, but cut back on its continental expansion plans when it became clear that the quality of its poultry supply could not be guaranteed. Woolworths has dabbled in Nigeria but, according to Ronak Gopaldas at Signal Risk in London, it failed due to a mixture of naivety and lack of cultural intelligence and empathy.

'South African businesses need to be a lot more streetwise in the way they operate in the rest of the continent. To be successful requires a few key elements – establishing the right local partner, understanding the lay of the land deeply, and developing the ability to be adaptive and agile in the face of volatility and uncertainty. Too many South African firms adopt a cookie-cutter approach which subsequently fails. Each country on the continent has its unique idiosyncrasies which renders the "copy-and-paste" approach that many corporates adopt unfit for purpose,' says Gopaldas, who also points to the fact that South Africans are still seen as condescending towards other Africans.

That is a weakness that must be addressed as the world looks at this continent as the last great global growth opportunity and countries position themselves to invest for growth, which demographic analysis suggests may come over the next two decades. In 2008, as the world was anxiously trying to work out the consequences of the global financial crisis, I returned from a course at New York's Columbia University, which had included deeply privileged access to some of America's best financial minds. I developed a reputation among a group of journalists from around the world of always asking the last question: 'What about an Africa strategy?' When I returned home I told the editor of *Finweek* magazine, for whom I was writing at the time, 'Uncle Sam doesn't give a damn.'

Those attitudes are now shifting. The venerable *Economist* in 2019 ran a cover story about the embassy-building boom across Africa, forecasting that it marked the beginning of a new period of opportunity for the continent. 'The extent of foreign engagement is unprecedented,' the magazine reported. 'Start with diplomacy. From 2010 to 2016 more than 320 embassies were opened in Africa, probably the biggest embassy-building boom anywhere, ever. Turkey alone opened 26. Last year India announced it would open 18. Military ties are deepening, too. America and France are lending muscle and technology to the struggle against jihadism in the Sahel. China is now the biggest arms seller to sub-Saharan Africa and has defence-technology ties with 45 countries. Russia has signed 19 military deals with African states since 2014. Oil-rich Arab states are building bases on the Horn of Africa and hiring African mercenaries.'

For South Africa, the value proposition is compelling. It has a strategic and geographic comparative advantage that can be leveraged to achieve success. Expanding trade and investment with the African continent is a key and underutilised economic lever for growth, especially given the subdued growth outlook domestically. With prospects for the grindingly slow African continental free-trade agreement gathering pace, local firms are well positioned to take advantage.

South Africa's biggest banks are betting on the growth opportunity. Standard Bank, which once had ideas of global growth and conducted operations in countries as diverse as Argentina, the UK and Russia, was forced to withdraw from these markets in the face of new capital requirements for international banks operating in foreign jurisdictions. It is now developing a network in Africa.

As part of its divestment from Absa, Barclays sold several of its existing businesses to the local group, which is also developing a strategy for growth on the continent. Instead of focusing on their domestic and regional markets, too many South African companies followed the ambitions of their managers and sought to expand into markets like Australia, where more than a handful of local companies have been taught lessons in abject humility. It has cost their shareholders billions. Now is the time to operate differently, for South African companies to play to their strengths and exploit their established networks on the continent.

But, says Gopaldas, for Africa to be successful, it needs its big economic dynamos to be firing: 'This is non-negotiable: getting the likes of South Africa, Nigeria and Egypt to grow sustainably and consistently will have a catalytic effect on the continent, spur regional integration and stimulate pan-African trade and investments, and ultimately lead to a more prosperous and stable Africa.'

South Africa cannot go over the edge and into the abyss. It cannot be allowed to fail. Its natural role as a leading African nation goes beyond the narrow self-interest and well-being of its own citizens. It remains the most advanced economy on the continent, and with that comes an enormous responsibility to resolve its domestic issues and ensure that it can grow not only to provide for its own citizens but also so that it can be part of a long-overdue African renaissance.

'The country offers a number of compelling comparative advantages to investors – most notably its infrastructure, financial-services sector, connectivity, and institutional strength,' says Gopaldas. 'In recent years, much of the shine has faded. A series of policy missteps, periodic bouts of xenophobia, a clumsy foreign policy as well as a marked deterioration in its business environment have seen the country lose significant ground to other nations.'

We are at risk, says the CEO of RMB, James Formby, of becoming 'a forgotten country' among investors. That prospect should have a chilling effect on all players in the economy.

Getting back to the point where the country is taken seriously as an investment destination will require considerable effort by business leaders and policy-makers alike. What is frustrating is that it really is not rocket science to lay the groundwork for a recovery in fortunes. President Cyril Ramaphosa's first international investment drive, instigated towards the end of 2018, was going well until the January 2019 breakdown in power supplies. That only lasted a week but it was enough to warn off potential investors eager to capitalise on the president's call for $100bn in foreign direct investment by 2023. They, like many others, took a wait-and-see approach only to have their concerns vindicated by the seeming inability of policy-makers to act swiftly to ameliorate the worst effects of the failing state-owned power supplier, Eskom.

The South African government knows it has a vast array of issues to resolve and has made some progress in tackling some of the most obviously off-putting and maddening missteps of the Zuma era. The visa requirements for unabridged birth certificates for minors visiting the country with their parents, which undermined tourism growth, have been relaxed. But it will take a far more concerted effort by South Africa to convince the world that it is a serious destination for real money. It needs to make urgent strides in guaranteeing power supply as well as providing certainty on a range of issues such as security of land tenure and labour regulations, all the while balancing this with the growing demands of a populace left on the economic periphery for far too long.

We, like other African countries, have been far too inwardly focused for decades past. This has led to a loss of a competitive advantage in a fast-moving world. The country needs urgently to become more competitive, enhance digital infrastructure, and improve skills levels to take advantage of the fourth industrial revolution, beyond paying mere lip service to the idea as a trendy turn of phrase.

Bizarrely, a crisis might just be what South Africa needs to force the hand of policy-makers to become more decisive. Crises that may accelerate a recovery following a collapse, however, hurt the most vulnerable in society in the short term and should be avoided. South Africa needs to pre-empt its crisis and it can do so only through action. Shocks can be used positively to enact reform. South Africa has had more than its fair share of those.

Ramaphoria was never going to last. It was an illusion, a brief respite after the Zuma years, before the reality of the damage wrought during the period of gross public mismanagement became clear. The deliberate destruction of the Scorpions, endorsed by the ANC elective conference at Polokwane in December 2007, which brought fraud-accused Jacob Zuma to power for what we now refer to as the 'lost decade', was a turning point for the country, which was only just beginning to emerge from the bloody fog of the apartheid era.

South Africa, perpetually on the edge of a self-made crisis of some description, came closer than ever before to throwing itself into the abyss at the ANC elective conference in December 2017. Just 179 people needed to vote differently in the battle for the leadership of the party, and the country would immediately have been downgraded to sub-investment level by all ratings agencies, and the brain drain already under way would have accelerated. We would not have had the numerous commissions of inquiry that have brought to light the gory details of a legion of abuses of the country's legal and economic systems. The Guptas would still be in Saxonwold, Tom Moyane at the helm of SARS, and the country's security services in the hands of the paranoid and the perpetually destructive. It could have been so much worse.

Consider what has been achieved in a relatively short period of time since then. South Africans have a far better idea today of the consequences of failed government and grotesque political mismanagement of a country. Institutions can operate for years before imploding, and that is why it was not apparent during the Zuma years that things were falling apart. When the collapse comes, however, it comes alarmingly quickly and hence the deluge of negative news flow in 2019 and no doubt beyond.

But the repair crew is in place. Tito Mboweni has taken charge at the National Treasury, restoring its place at the centre of the economy and of policy-making. Reserve Bank governor Lesetja Kganyago has correctly refused to bow to populist pressures to cut interest rates so as to give the economy a short-term consumption-led boost. As governor of the Reserve Bank, he was voted by industry peers as the world's best for standing firm against nefarious self-interest, dominated by calls to nationalise the Bank. Former Eskom chairman Reuel Khoza, at the helm of Eskom when power was cheap and plentiful, has been strategically placed in charge of the Public Investment Corporation as the guardian of R2tn in civil service pension monies at a time when politicians are looking for quick and easy access to new sources of ready cash ripe for plunder.

We have also started to see the earliest stages of charges being laid against once-untouchable politicians by the fragile National

Prosecuting Authority – another institution raped of talent during the Zuma years. Edward Kieswetter, an old-fashioned ANC stalwart, has been brought by Ramaphosa from the brink of retirement to reignite SARS, the national tax authority, and rebuild its capacity to collect the money needed to drive the country's recovery. By the time this book is published, South Africa will have an idea of the strategy of André de Ruyter, the new CEO at Eskom, the power utility being held together by a combination of prayer, hope and sticky tape. De Ruyter, the man who ran Sasol's massive coal business and should have taken over from Pat Davies as CEO of Sasol at the time the board went for David Constable, the international candidate who drove the strategy behind the ill-fated Lake Charles project, was chosen to fix the broken power utility from a list of 142 potential candidates. The fact that 142 people put up their hands to be considered for the gargantuan task of fixing Eskom tells you all you need to know about the extraordinary level of self-belief that South Africans have.

Despite its ongoing difficulties in providing adequate power, the internal governance clean-up at Eskom is under way. Several high-profile culprits have been dismissed and face potential prosecution for frauds perpetrated on their watch while the company is tightening up on procurement and other weaknesses that have helped in effect to bankrupt the utility.

The commissions of inquiry into state capture instituted by the president have been awful to watch. A friend once described how his wife had made him watch a DVD of his undergoing an operation during which his heart stopped and had to be restarted. It was a step too far for my friend, who is otherwise a fan of reality

TV shows. But watching the Zondo Commission into state capture and the Mpati Commission into the failings of the PIC as well as the SARS inquiry was almost too much to bear. The blatant disregard shown by an elected political elite for the people who put them in power is there for all to see. Like any therapy, one has to confront one's own demons in order to heal. South Africa has been through the equivalent of my friend watching himself die on the operating table. He had great doctors (funded by expensive medical aid) and recovered. Cyril Ramaphosa is banking on the fact that his interventions can have the same impact on the country.

Kieswetter has succeeded in clearing out much of the rot at the head of SARS. Moyane is gone, as are some of his less salubrious henchmen and -women, including the former 'protect-me-from-yourself' head of IT, Mmamathe Makhekhe-Mokhuane. The recovery of the NPA has been frustratingly slow, as those being shifted out by the new national director of public prosecutions, Shamila Batohi, have used every legal avenue, at state expense, to preserve their positions. If only they'd put as much effort into prosecuting crime as they did into trying to keep their jobs, they might still have been employed. The Scorpions are a footnote in the history books, but the Hawks are under new management too and early signs show that General Godfrey Lebeya is on the side of restoring the integrity and capability of the state. It will be good to see some private-sector prosecutions accompany the inevitable list of public-sector dockets that must materialise in 2020.

The long-overdue decisions to place SAA under business rescue and the railway utility Prasa under administration are encouraging signs that the taps of endless public cash are gradually being closed. State-owned entity mismanagement and the role of politicians in board appointments and in the deployment of the corrupt, incompetent and incapable to positions of authority over multi-billion-rand balance sheets may be coming to an end as the country faces financial calamity. It's just a pity that things had to get so bad before the changes came and the causes of many of the problems could be addressed.

Businesses exist to solve problems. At least that's how they start out.

Some become corrupted, some fail, but those that survive exist because they address a human need or desire. You had no idea that you 'needed' a smart device before Steve Jobs told you that you would – in a digital world, life is far more complicated without a machine to connect you to the world than with one. How many apps did you use on the first version of the first smartphone you bought, compared to the number you use now? Odds are that you use just a fraction of what it is capable of doing, but the tool that is the smart device is fundamentally changing the way we communicate, transact, run businesses, capture and store memories, and even entertain ourselves. Gone are the sets of *Encyclopaedia Britannica*, the SLR camera, the handycam, the photo album, the hi-fi, the TV, the radio, the newspaper subscription, the library card, the pack of cards, the chess set, the plane tickets, the need to visit a bank or a travel agent. You don't even need to attend a church service if you don't want to – you can stream it to a device in the palm of your hand.

So many of the problems our country faces are deeply rooted in structural inequality, which means that you either get a head start in life or start with your feet firmly set in concrete. Yes, this is true anywhere. But it is accentuated in South Africa, where recent Oxfam figures show the wealthiest 1% of the population own two-thirds of its wealth, and the top 10% some 93% of the wealth. Sure, you could do a once-off grab and distribute the proceeds, but the money wouldn't go particularly far, nor would it last particularly long, and before you knew it, we'd be mired in a Venezuela-style morass.

One of the key reasons why South Africa has not imploded into a suppurating heap is that the corporate sector, the previous generation of start-ups, has provided a backbone for jobs, taxes and growth. The business community is not nearly as influential as it would like to be and certainly nowhere as influential as its most vociferous critics claim when it comes to shaping the economy. It does, however, have a big impact when it comes to driving growth opportunities for smaller companies through its power of procurement and the fact that it provides the base for the country's pension wealth.

The country has too few home-grown companies and the economy is far too concentrated in too few hands, but the fact remains that without the jobs created and the taxes paid by today's corporates, many of them in start-up mode themselves 30 to 40 years ago, we would be nowhere.

While many people despair about today's social, political and economic travails, the reality is that if the founders of some of today's biggest corporates had waited for certainty so as to make a lower-risk entry into the economy, they would have waited forever.

Next time you go to a conference and someone tells you how

tough life is and how we live in a 'VUCA' world, hurl a stream of abuse in their direction. VUCA, one of those acronyms devised by consultants looking to distil the deeply complex into a single 'take-away' soundbite – it stands for Volatile, Uncertain, Complex and Ambiguous – has been hijacked more recently and many of its proponents nowadays believe that the world and its economies are in the worst state for decades. To suggest that the world, and in particular South Africa, are more VUCA today than at any other time in modern history is ludicrous.

Try telling that to the soldiers who landed on the Normandy beaches or fought in Vietnam, people who endured the indignities of apartheid, were separated by the Berlin Wall, or endured multiple recessions that saw economies fail and jobs lost. In the same way, recent surveys presume to point towards a collapse in business and consumer confidence in South Africa that exceeds that of the 1980s, with PW Botha's Rubicon speech and the debt standstill. You do have to wonder whatever happened to perspective.

South Africans suffer from considerable bouts of recency bias.

Consumer and business confidence are indeed at multi-year lows, but there is no way South Africa is anywhere close to the levels of anxiety that prevailed in the run-up to the 1994 elections when Chris Hani was killed and it seemed uncertain whether the political transition could happen in relative peace. We picked ourselves up from that mess. Surely we can do it again.

For me, that profound sense of the possible comes from the privilege of meeting some of the most interesting and committed problem-solvers you will find anywhere on earth and seeing the light in their eyes as they set about changing the world. It comes from meeting people like Cyril Ramaphosa, Tito Mboweni, Reuel Khoza and Lesetja Kganyago, who would far rather be doing something else than mopping up the mess left by a cabal who set out to destroy the country for personal gain. They, like all of us, are imperfect, but they have a commitment to making the country realise at least some of its potential.

Right now, things feel bad, but we are experiencing the fear and uncertainty of the current environment, which is far from ideal, though it is also nothing like the madness of the past.

The belief that life is worse now than it was in the past is a considerable constraint on progress. There are those who see problems as debilitating and impossible to resolve, while others see problems as an opportunity to solve an issue and build a solution. Some of them are expanding their enterprises, suggesting that with the correct application and with proper incentives in place, many problems can be solved by entrepreneurs and entrepreneurial thinking.

It seems ridiculous that at least some modern business teaching is derived from a book that is 2,500 years old. In *The Art of War*, Sun Tzu wrote: 'In the midst of chaos, there is also opportunity.' Perhaps it is because Michael Douglas's character Gordon Gekko in the legendary 1980s movie *Wall Street* quotes the ancient text so liberally that it has once again become popular as a basic text for 21st-century business. Japanese businesses have been using it as a basis for strategy for decades and it has grown in popularity in the West more recently.

Great problem-solvers see the future differently from the rest of us. They see the problem as an opportunity rather than as an obstacle. There is an upside to down. In South Africa we tend to get stuck at the obstacle.

If you want problems, you are in the right place. South Africa in 2020 is fraught with problems. Many find them insurmountable and overwhelming. Many are fed up dealing with corrupt bureaucracies and rent-seeking thugs who look to assert their authority for personal gain. That is all very real. But the tough environment also means that competition is kept out and the problems that present themselves become problems waiting to be solved.

South Africa is full of opportunities for those with the skills and the desire to get things done. Far too much of our energy is wasted on the bloodsuckers, crooks, scoundrels and vagabonds who dominate our screens, newspaper headlines and braai discussions. If we spent more time looking for solutions to the problems rather than focusing on the problems and those that cause them, we'd be far better off.

Mark Barnes resigned from the South African Post Office in July 2019 over a difference of opinion on strategy with government, the shareholder of the institution that he had led back from the brink of collapse. Fed up with his own posturing in a weekly column in *Business Day*, he had offered his services to government and took on a five-year contract to turn the Post Office around. He would have liked to complete his mission, which was to hand over a fully integrated, 21st-century logistics and financial-services entity built on the experience of global best practice, but his insistence that Postbank, the deposit-taking institution owned by the Post Office be converted into a fully-fledged state-owned bank within the existing unit, was a step too far for government. Government wants to keep them separate.

There was a risk, say some, that Barnes had done a bit too well and was making state failures in the other entities it owns look even worse. It's a cynical view. But in an environment in which SAA was finally placed in business rescue, Prasa under administration, and Eskom for the first time descended into Stage 6 load-shedding, pushing the economy from minuscule growth into its first self-imposed recession since 1994, they may have a point.

Far from being embittered, Barnes was philosophical, and no sooner had he stepped down from the Post Office than he expressed a desire to continue to support government wherever he could. 'We've got to get over ourselves and understand that together we are going to win, and disparate we are going to fail. It's about adding skill sets together so that eventually and finally we can start to trust one another, despite the fact that we come from completely different backgrounds, different places, different profiles. That we have different things to bring to the party. We need to hold hands. Trust one another.'

Remember the note beneath the grubby light switch in my children's classroom?

Dear Optimists, Pessimists and Realists,
While you were arguing about the level of the water in the glass,
I drank it.
Regards
The Opportunist

Well, there's another more defeatist note pinned to the wall above a urinal in the toilets at a Cape Town food market:

Smile. These are the good old days you will be dreaming about one day.

If that is indeed the case, we are in more trouble than I feared.

It was my job to thank Bill and Hillary Clinton for travelling to South Africa for a massive conference in 2018. She'd just published her book about her shock defeat by Donald Trump in the race for the US presidency and Bill, at the age of 72, was showing signs of age. I needed a memorable parting shot from the former US president.

'Any advice for us, Mr President, before you go?'

He paused for a moment. 'Don't screw it up.'

Don't screw it up, indeed.

Acknowledgements

If you enjoy this book it is due to the generosity of spirit exhibited to me by so many people over many years. There are too many to mention here, but it is thanks to the wisdom, patience and counsel of a great number of mentors from many disciplines in the complex world of high finance that I survived a baptism of fire to gain a foothold in financial journalism. I am eternally grateful to each one of you. To those mavericks starting out and those who are slowing down after decades of building extraordinary, globally competitive businesses in a tough and often-hostile environment, those who answer the phone and return their emails – thank you. To those who don't, that's also fine. You, too, are an inspiration. Otherwise the call would never have been made in the first place.

South Africa needs more inspiring stories. The stories Owen Muzambi heard on the radio inspired him out of homelessness and to take charge of his future. Never underestimate the power of stories. In a country bereft of optimism and hope, we must always ensure that the truth prevails. We must never suppress the negativity. But few things are all bad. If you look hard enough you will find extraordinary tales of people succeeding against considerable odds, and we need to seek out and tell more of those stories.

If you hate this book, blame Pavlo Phitidis at Aurik, who wanted to share some of the agony a writer goes through in the process of delivering a manuscript, as he completed his best-seller *Sweat, Scale, $ell*. He sat me down with Pan Macmillan MD Terry Morris, who made sense of a hastily drawn spider-gram and commissioned a book with a completely different, and unprintable title. Thanks to her and publisher Andrea Nattrass for their patient cajoling, to editor Russell Martin for spending his December holiday wading through the first draft and making it readable, as well as to Wesley Thompson for his detailed proofreading. And to the rest of the remarkable team that takes the work of writers and gets it to readers – thank you.

To those who read early-draft chapters and gave support and encouragement, to the many contributors who generously gave of their time and energy to add insights and fresh perspectives – thank you.

To my dad, who at 92 plays at least two rounds of golf a week, has a spring in his step and a twinkle in his good eye, thanks for not taking seriously my primary school headmaster Ian Patterson's assertion that I'd never make it to university.

To Catherine, my muse and business manager – this would not have happened without your constant backing.

Bad news – I have an idea for the next book.